THE WORLD OF
Music

THE WORLD OF MUSIC

Nicola Barber
and Mary Mure

SILVER BURDETT PRESS
Parsippany, New Jersey

This book is dedicated to Lucy Ellen Taylor.

First published in 1995 by Evans Brothers Limited, 2A Portman Mansions, Chiltern Street, London W1M 1LE

Published in the United States in 1995 by Silver Burdett Press,
A Simon and Schuster Company
299 Jefferson Road
Parsippany, NJ 07054

Printed by GRAFO, in Spain.
10 9 8 7 6 5 4 3 2 1

Library of Congress Cataloging-in-Publication Data

Barber, Nicola.
The world of music/Nicola Barber and Mary Mure.
p. cm.
Includes index.
ISBN 0-382-39116-0 (LSB) ISBN 0-382-39117-9 (SC)
1. Musical instruments—Juvenile literature. 2. Music—History and criticism—Juvenile literature. 3. Music—Theory, Elementary. I. Mure, Mary. II. Title
ML3928.B37 1995
780—dc20 95-1394
CIP
AC MN

Acknowledgments

With thanks to Helen Drew for reading the manuscript.
For permission to reproduce copyright material, the author and publishers gratefully acknowledge the following:
Cover (clockwise from top left) Robert Harding Picture Library, VCL/Telegraph Colour Library, Sarah Errington/The Hutchison Library, Gavin Hellier/Robert Harding Picture Library (back cover) The Bridgeman Art Library
page 8 (top) Robert Harding Picture Library, (bottom) The Bridgeman Art Library; **page 9** (top) Spectrum Colour Library (bottom) Laister Dickson Ltd; **page 10** (top) Giraudon, The Bridgeman Art Library, (bottom) Barry Mayes, Life File; **page 11** (top) Jonathan Fisher, Performing Arts Library, (bottom) SH & DH Cavanaugh, Robert Harding Picture Library; **page 12** Giraudon, The Bridgeman Art Library; **page 13** (top) British Museum, The Bridgeman Art Library, (bottom) Alvis Upitis, The Image Bank; **page 14** (top) Resource Foto, Redferns, (bottom) Tony Russell, Redferns; **page 15** Robert Harding Picture Library; **page 16** (top) Trustees of Berkeley Castle, The Bridgeman Art Library, (bottom) Robert Harding Picture Library; **page 17** (top) David Hughes, Robert Harding Picture Library, (bottom) R Ian Lloyd, The Hutchison Library; **page 18** Towneley Hall Art Gallery & Museum, The Bridgeman Art Library; **page 19** (top) Clive Barda, Performing Arts Library, (bottom) Odile Noel, Redferns; **page 20** Dulwich Picture Library, The Bridgeman Art Library; **page 21** Clive Barda, Performing Arts Library; **page 23** The Hutchison Library; **page 24** (top) Victoria & Albert Museum, The Bridgeman Art Library, (bottom) Mary Evans Picture Library; **page 25** (top) Mary Evans Picture Library, (bottom) Jeremy Hoare, Life File; **page 26** Gavin Hellier, Robert Harding Picture Library; **page 27** (left) James McCormick, Performing Arts Library, (right) The Hutchison Library; **page 28** (top) Archiv für Kunste und Geschichte, (bottom) Werner Forman Archive; **page 29** (top) The Bridgeman Art Library (bottom) P Trummer, The Image Bank; **page 30** (top) Nigel Blythe, Robert Harding Picture Library, (bottom) e.t. archive; **page 31** (left) JG Fuller, The Hutchison Library, (right) ZEFA; **page 32** The Bridgeman Art Library; **page 33** (top) Alan Becker, The Image Bank, (bottom) David Redfern, Redferns; **page 35** (top) Tim Megarry, Robert Harding Picture Library, (bottom) Odile Noel, Redferns; **page 36** Juliet Highet, Life File; **page 37** (top) Jeremy Hoare, Life File, (bottom) Trip; **page 38** Mowy Jeliffe, Trip; **page 39** (top) Juliet Highet, Trip, (bottom) Bernard Gerrard, The Hutchison Library; **page 40** James McCormick, Performing Arts Library; **page 41** David Redfern, Redferns; **page 42** (bottom left) Michael MacIntyre, The Hutchison Library, (bottom right) Richard Powers, Life File; **page 43** (top left) GM Wilkins, Robert Harding Picture Library, (top right) Peter Palmer, Trip, (bottom) Mike Maidment, Life File; **page 44** Queen Productions Ltd; **page 46** Bettmann, Range Pictures Ltd; **page 47** James McCormick, Performing Arts Library; **page 48** (top) David Hughes, Robert Harding Picture Library, (bottom) Edward Parker, The Hutchison Library; **page 49** Colorific!; **page 50** Mary Evans Picture Library; **page 51** (top) Bibliothèque de l'Arsenal, The Bridgeman Art Library, (bottom) Harrogate Museums and Art Gallery, The Bridgeman Art Library; **page 52** (top) Bettmann, Range Pictures Ltd, (bottom) Hermitage, The Bridgeman Art Library; **page 54** (top) The Bridgeman Art Library, (bottom) British Library, The Bridgeman Art Library; **page 55** Museo de Firenze Con'era, The Bridgeman Art Library; **page 56** (top) The Bridgeman Art Library, (bottom) Pushkin Museum, The Bridgeman Art Library; **page 57** (top) Church of St Agostino, The Bridgeman Art Library, (bottom) Robert Harding Picture Library; **page 59** (top) Mary Evans Picture Library, (middle) Bettmann, Range Pictures Ltd, (bottom) Mary Evans Picture Library; **page 61** (top and middle) Mary Evans Picture Library, (bottom) The Bridgeman Art Library; **page 62** (top) Mary Evans Picture Library, (bottom) Adam Woolfitt, Robert Harding Picture Library; **page 63** Historisches Museum der Stadt, The Bridgeman Art Library; **page 64** (top) Giraudon, The Bridgeman Art Library, (bottom) Whitford & Hughes, The Bridgeman Art Library; **page 65** Mary Evans Picture Library; **page 66** Mary Evans Picture Library; **page 67** (top) Caroline Field, Life File, (middle) Bettmann, Range Pictures Ltd, (bottom) Clive Barda, Performing Arts Library; **page 68** (top) Popperfoto, (bottom) Clive Barda, Performing Arts Library; **page 69** (top and middle) Bettmann, Range Pictures Ltd, (bottom) Juliet Highet, Trip; **page 70** (top) Mary Evans Picture Library, (bottom) Helene Rogers, Trip; **page 71** (top) Arthur Jumper, Life File, (bottom) Graham Harison, Telegraph Colour Library; **page 72** (top) Sarah Errington, The Hutchison Library, (bottom) Mary Evans Picture Library; **page 73** D Saunders, Trip; **page 74** (top) Mary Evans Picture Library, (bottom) Michael St Maur Sheil, Colorific!; **page 75** (top) Robert Phillips, The Image Bank, (bottom) Alvis Upitis, The Image Bank; **page 78** Mary Evans Picture Library; **page 80** P Ward, Telegraph Colour Library; **page 81** VCL, Telegraph Colour Library; **page 82** VCL, Telegraph Colour Library; **page 83** Bill Varie, The Image Bank; **page 87** Archiv für Kunst und Geshichte, Berlin; **page 88** (top) Bettman, Range Pictures Ltd.; (bottom) Historisches Museum Der Stadt, Vienna, Bridgeman Art Library; **page 89** (top) Arthur Kaufman, The Bridgeman Art Library; (bottom) Bettman, Range Pictures Ltd; **page 90** (top and bottom) Bettman, Range Pictures Ltd; **page 91** (top) Mary Evans Picture Library, (bottom) Archiv für Kunst und Geschichte, Berlin, Bridgeman Art Library.

Contents

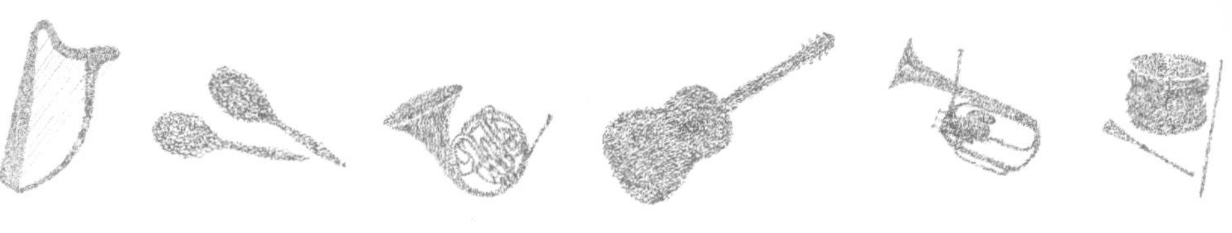

This 15th-century illustrated manuscript shows how music was written down in those days.

Introduction

This book is divided into eleven chapters. Chapters one to three tell you about musical instruments from all over the world. Some will be familiar, and some you may never have heard of before. In these chapters you will find boxes about instruments of the orchestra and some other well-known instruments that you might be learning to play, such as the piano and the guitar. Chapter four gives you information about electronic instruments, old and very new. Chapters five to eight explore the history of music in the Western world from 1100 up to the present day, while chapter nine is about the music of people all over the world–working songs and music for entertainment.

A 19th-century painting of Johann Strauss conducting an orchestra at a court ball.

Music is enjoyed all over the world. These musicians come from Bali.

Finally, chapters ten and eleven introduce you to how music is put together and how it is written down.

Throughout the book there are **Key facts** notes, which point out important information.

If there are any musical words that you find difficult in this book, you may find them in the Glossary of musical terms at the end of the book (see pages 84–87). If you want to know about a particular composer, you can look up his or her name in the Glossary of composers (see pages 88–91).

Most of all have fun reading about music!

Key facts

Pitch: the pitch of a note is how high or low it is.
Volume: the volume of a note is how loud or soft it is.

Today's music has developed with the technological world. Here Peter Gabriel performs in concert playing a variety of electronic instruments.

Please note!

In the instrument boxes you will see a keyboard, which shows the pitch range of the instruments in the box. Middle C is colored in bright red.

Listen out!

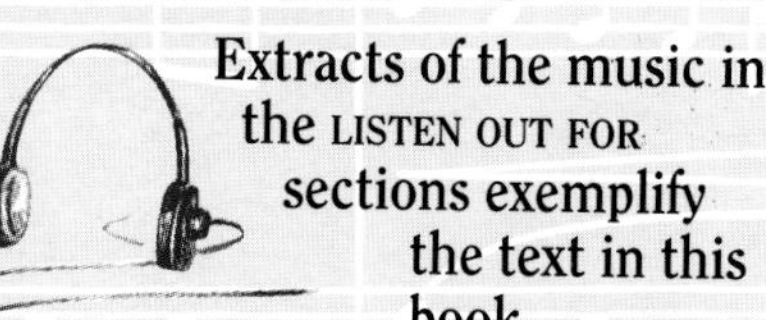

Extracts of the music in the LISTEN OUT FOR sections exemplify the text in this book.

Instruments with strings

An ancient Egyptian wall painting shows a harpist entertaining two listeners. This picture is more than 4,000 years old.

THERE ARE MANY DIFFERENT WAYS of playing strings. Sometimes the strings are plucked with the fingers or with a hard piece of plastic or wood called a plectrum. Sometimes the strings are played with a bow. There is also a group of instruments that have their strings hit by beaters or hammers. But whether the strings are plucked, bowed, or hit, the end result is that they vibrate.

Key facts

Instruments that use strings to make sound are called chordophones.

Your ears hear the vibrations of the strings as a musical note. The pitch of the note sounded by the strings is affected by the thickness of the string, its length, and how tightly it is stretched. If you look at the strings on a guitar, you will see that the strings with the lower pitches are slightly thicker than those with higher pitches. The strings of the double bass are far thicker and longer than those of the violin. As a result, the double bass plays some of the deepest notes in the orchestra, and the violin plays some of the highest.

Once the violin is strung, the four strings must be tuned using tuning pegs.

Tuning strings

The strings on a musical instrument are tightened until they sound the correct pitches for that instrument. Tightening the strings in this way is called tuning an instrument. Different instruments have different numbers of strings, which all have to be tuned to the right pitch. A modern guitar has six strings; a violin has four strings. The strings on both these instruments are tuned by winding the loose end of the string around a tuning

Key facts

The pitch of a string is determined by three things:
1. how thin or thick the string is: a thin string has a higher pitch than a thick one.
2. how tightly stretched the string is: a tight string has a higher pitch than a looser one.
3. how long the string is: a short string has a higher pitch than a long one.

peg. The player turns the tuning peg in its hole until the string is tight enough to sound the correct pitch.

The guitar has six strings, so the guitar player can play six different notes by simply plucking the strings with one hand. But it is possible to play more than one note on each string. This is done by pressing each string down against the fingerboard with the fingers of the other hand. If you press one of the strings down, you make the vibrating part of that string shorter. You can change the length of the vibrating part of the string by pressing the string down in different places. This is called "stopping" the string. The guitar has bars called frets on its fingerboard. These show players where to put their fingers to sound different notes. The violin does not have frets. Violinists must learn whether their fingers are in the right place by listening carefully to the pitch of the note.

The fingerboard of the guitar has thin strips of metal called frets to show players where to put their fingers.

Resonators

The first string instruments were probably musical bows, developed from hunting bows. Musical bows were simply made from a length of string, either vegetable fiber or twisted animal hairs tied at both ends to a flexible stick. They were played by plucking or bowing the string. But early musicians soon discovered that they could increase the amount of noise produced by the bow if it were held against a hollow object, such as a coconut shell or a gourd (a dried vegetable shell). The vibrations made by the bow itself produced only a faint sound. But when the vibrations were picked up by the air inside the shell or gourd, the sound became much louder. The shell or gourd was acting as a resonator. Today musical bows are still played in Africa

This homemade instrument has two strings attached to tuning pegs, a bow, and a resonator made from a gourd.

The hollow body of the violin acts as a resonator to make the strings sound much louder.

and Asia, and a tin can is often used as a resonator.

Modern instruments have resonators, too. The strings of a violin would produce a feeble sound if they were not connected by the bridge and sound post to the front and back of the body of the violin. The hollow body of the violin acts as the resonator, picking up the vibrations of the strings and making their sound louder.

Plucking strings

One of the stories, or myths, that has come down to us from the ancient Greeks tells the story of Orpheus. In one part of the myth, Orpheus plays a lyre so beautifully that he persuades the god of the underworld to allow him to take his wife, Eurydice, back from the land of the dead. Unfortunately Orpheus cannot resist stealing a look at Euridyce as he leads her back from the underworld, although he has been forbidden to do so. As soon as he looks, Eurydice disappears once again.

The lyre that Orpheus played so beautifully is a very old instrument that was known even before ancient Greek times. Both the lyre and the harp were played as long as 4,000 years ago by the people of Sumer, the region that is present-day Iraq. We know this because both types of instruments have been found buried in the tombs of the kings of Sumer. Pictures of musicians playing harps and lyres also appear in the wall paintings of the ancient Egyptians.

Both the lyre and harp are played by plucking the strings. The lyre has strings attached to a resonator at one end and a crossbar at the other end. The strings are all the same length, but they are tuned by turning pegs on the crossbar. The harp has diagonal strings, attached to the resonator on one side and the neck of the harp on the

This Roman mosaic shows Orpheus playing his lyre.

A copy of a bull-headed lyre found in the ancient city of Ur in Sumeria. It would have been played around 2500 BC.

other. The strings are different lengths, and there are usually far more strings than on the lyre. Today, lyres are still played in parts of Africa, especially to accompany singing for wedding parties. Harps are played by people all over the world, and the modern harp has become an orchestral instrument.

The harp

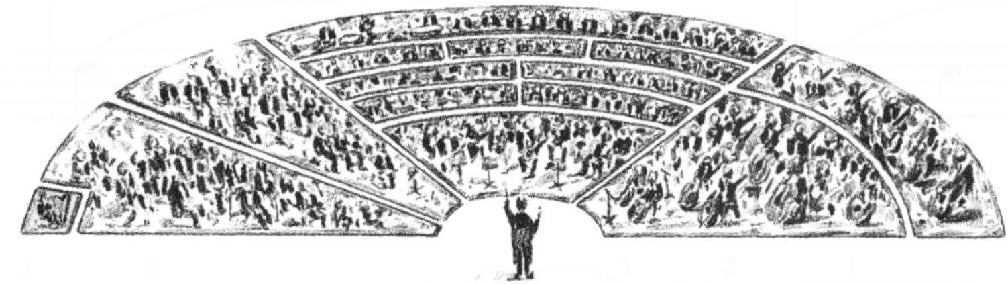

The harpist often sits behind the violins. Sometimes there are two harps in an orchestra.

The harp has the widest range of notes of all the orchestral instruments.

LISTEN OUT FOR the harp in: **Mozart's *Concerto for flute and harp***; Tchaikovsky's 'Waltz of the flowers' from *The Nutcracker Suite*.

THE HARP has 47 strings. Before playing the harp, the harpist must tune all the strings using the tuning pegs on the neck of the harp. The harp has seven pedals which change the pitch of the strings when they are pressed.

The harp is leaned against the harpist's shoulder, with one hand on each side of the strings.

The strings of the vina can be plucked with long fingernails. This musician is using a plectrum instead.

Indian strings

The oldest of the many string instruments played in India is called the vina (see left). The vina is mostly played in southern India. It is mentioned in one of the Vedas, holy books of the Hindu religion, which date back about 3,500 years. Vina players use their specially long fingernails to pluck the strings running along the fingerboard. The vina has two soundboxes, often made from gourds and beautifully decorated.

The sitar

The sitar is probably the best-known of all Indian instruments. The sitar has extra strings that give it a beautiful, shimmery sound. These are called sympathetic strings, and they lie underneath the main strings. When the player plucks the main strings to play a melody, the sympathetic strings vibrate, too. Even though they are not plucked, the sympathetic strings can be tuned by tightening or loosening the pegs along the side of the fingerboard of the sitar. A sitar usually has seven main strings, and between 11 and 19 sympathetic strings.

You can hear the sound of the sitar in the accompaniment to the song "Norwegian Wood" by the Beatles. The Beatles was the first pop group to try out different instruments together with the usual rock lineup of electric guitars and drum kit (see page 41).

Ravi Shankar is a famous sitar player. He was born in India in 1920.

Three Japanese kotos played by women wearing their traditional dress, kimonos.

Zithers from the East

An oriental zither has strings stretched along a board that acts as the resonator. The strings are plucked with the fingers or with a plectrum. Simple zithers are found all over the world, but some of the most ancient are the zithers of China and Japan. The Chinese zither is called the qin. In China, a qin was found buried in a tomb that was 2,000 years old. The qin still had all 25 of its strings. Modern qins have seven strings.

The Japanese zither is called the koto. The koto was originally modeled on the qin, and it came to Japan about A.D. 600. There are many traditional Japanese stories that mention the koto. In *The Tale of the Genji,* Prince Genji is a skillful koto player. He falls in love with a beautiful girl who also plays the koto, but they are forced to part. He leaves her, promising to be as true and constant as the middle string of his koto. (The middle string is always tuned to the same note.) Eventually they are reunited. The first sounds that Genji hears as he rides out to greet his beloved are those of her koto.

The koto has 13 strings, made from silk (or sometimes nylon). Underneath each string lies a small piece of wood called a bridge. The koto player moves these bridges up and down the string to alter the length of the vibrating part of the string, changing the pitch.

Key facts

Sympathetic strings are not played. Instead they lie underneath the main strings and vibrate when these strings are played.

This string instrument from China, called a p'i p'a, is plucked.

Lutes and guitars

This miniature painting by Nicholas Hilliard shows Queen Elizabeth I playing the lute.

A lute has a hollow body, which is the resonator, and a neck sticking out from the body. The strings run from the bottom of the resonator to the other end of the neck. In Europe lutes became very popular in the 1600s and 1700s. The type of lute played during this period had a deep, pear-shaped back. The number of strings varied because there were many different lute designs, but they were often arranged in pairs. The strings were attached to tuning pegs in a box that was often bent right back. The strings in each pair were tuned to the same pitch, so that when they were plucked together they gave a strong note. The lute was often used to accompany songs.

The guitar was also used as an accompanying instrument. It was very popular all over Europe, but particularly in Spain. In the 19th and 20th centuries, many Spanish composers have written solo music for the guitar, including Andrés Segovia, Manuel de Falla, and Joãquin Rodrigo. Guitar design has continued to change as the guitar has been adapted for use in jazz, rock, folk, and pop music (see page 45).

The guitar is especially popular in Spain. It is used to accompany flamenco dancers.

The guitar

The modern guitar has six strings, tuned to the notes low E, A, D, G, B and high E.

This musician is playing a classical guitar.

LISTEN OUT FOR the guitar in: Rodrigo's *Concierto de Aranjuez* and de Falla's *Homenaje,* "Le tombeau de Claude Debussy."

This is the classical guitar's range.

A girl from Thailand plays a two-stringed fiddle using a bow, which is threaded through the strings.

Bowing and scraping

One of the most important musical instruments in the orchestra is the violin, a string instrument that is not (usually) plucked, but played with a bow. The violin is popular because it is a very expressive instrument. It can be played softly and sweetly or fast and very dramatically. The strings of the violin are sometimes plucked–this is called pizzicato. But the four strings of the violin are most usually played with a bow made from horse hair. The violin has a long history, and many different kinds of violins are still played in various parts of the world.

Another name for the violin is the fiddle. The earliest fiddles known in Europe were small pear-shaped

The part of the violin bow that is drawn across the strings is made from strands of horse hair.

Antonio Stradivari in his workshop at Cremona, painted by Edgar Bundy in the 19th century.

instruments that were descended from an Arab fiddle called a rebab. These early fiddles were called rebecs. Instruments that look very similar to the rebec are still played in Bulgaria and Greece. Another early fiddle was the lira da braccio. This looked more like the modern violin and was held against the left shoulder. But the lira da braccio had five strings on the fingerboard and two extra strings that ran by the side of the fingerboard. These two strings are called drone strings. They were attached to tuning pegs so they could be tuned, but they could not be stopped by the player's fingers because they did not run over the fingerboard. Instead they were played as a drone–a long continuous note underneath the main melody.

The violin as we know it was first made in about 1550, and its appearance has changed very little since then. One of the greatest violin-makers was an Italian called Antonio Stradivari (1644–1737). He worked in Cremona in northern Italy, and above his house today there is a sign that says that it was he "who brought the violin to perfection." Some original Stradivari violins have survived, and when these are sold, they fetch huge amounts of money. Stradivari also made violas and cellos.

The pocket fiddle

The kit was a tiny violin, small enough to fit into a pocket. This was exactly what it was designed for. In the 18th century, dancing masters went from house to house to teach the latest dance. The kit provided the music for these dancing lessons. When the lesson was finished, the dancing master put his kit in the pocket of his greatcoat and went to his next lesson.

The violin and viola

The violin has four strings, tuned to the notes G, D, A, and E. In the orchestra the violins are divided into firsts and seconds. The viola is slightly bigger than the violin and has a richer tone. Because viola music does not fit very well on the treble or bass clefs, the viola has its own clef called the alto clef. In the alto clef the middle line on the staff is Middle C. The violas sit almost directly in front of the conductor.

LISTEN OUT FOR the violin in most orchestral pieces—composers often use the violins to play the main tunes. The violin is the solo instrument in: Mendelssohn's Violin Concerto; Bach's Concerto for Two Violins; Brahms's Violin Concerto.

LISTEN OUT FOR the viola in: Bach's *Brandenburg* Concerto no. 6; Mozart's *Sinfonia Concertante;* Berlioz's *Harold in Italy.*

This instrument is placed between the jaw and shoulder, when played.

The violin's range and position are shown in red; the viola is shown in blue; the cello in yellow and the double bass in purple.

The cello and double bass are balanced on the ground and played in front of the player.

The cello and double bass

The cello has four strings tuned one octave below the strings of the viola. The cellos sit to the right of the conductor. The double bass has four strings as well. Because the double bass plays such low notes, its music is written one octave higher than the note actually sounds. The double basses sit behind the cellos in the orchestra.

LISTEN OUT FOR the cello in: Dvořák's Cello Concerto; Saint-Saëns's "The Swan" from *Carnival of the Animals;* Lloyd Webber's *Variations* (after Paganini's *Caprice in A Minor*).

LISTEN OUT FOR the bass player plucking the strings in many jazz pieces. You can hear the double bass in: Saint-Saëns's "The Elephant" from *Carnival of the Animals;* Beethoven's Ninth Symphony (beginning of last movement); Schubert's *Trout* Quintet.

Keyboard string instruments

This 17th-century painting shows a young woman playing the clavichord, an instrument similar to the harpsichord.

If you look inside a piano, you will see rows of levers, hammers, and dampers. Behind them you will see the piano strings. The pianist plays the strings by pressing a key on the keyboard. The key operates a lever to move a hammer that strikes a string. So even though the pianist does not actually touch the string to sound a note, the piano, and other keyboard instruments with strings, can be classed as string instruments.

The harpsichord

The harpsichord is an older keyboard instrument than the piano. A type of "harpsichord" was probably made as early as the 14th century, but it became well-known in the 17th century. When the harpsichord player strikes a key on the keyboard, the key moves a piece of quill (or plastic) called a plectrum. The plectrum plucks a string, making the string vibrate. The plucked strings of the harpsichord give a light, even sound. This sound was ideal for making music in the grand houses of Europe to a small audience. But when public concerts began in the late 18th century (see page 58), musicians wanted an instrument with more power.

Hitting strings

The piano is not the only instrument that is played by hitting strings. The cimbalom is a Hungarian instrument with strings stretched over a soundbox. The strings are hit by hammers with ends padded with cotton that are held in the player's hands. The cimbalom was traditionally played by Hungarian gypsies.

The pianoforte

The name pianoforte comes from the Italian *piano e forte*, meaning "soft and loud." If the pianist plays the notes on the keyboard gently, the piano produces a quiet sound. If the pianist strikes the notes with more force, then the sound is louder. In this way the piano was a more expressive instrument than the harpsichord, and it became a very popular solo instrument in the 19th century. The earliest pianofortes were made in the early 1700s by an Italian harpsichord-maker called Bartolomeo Cristofori.

The piano

There are many pieces written for solo piano.

LISTEN OUT FOR the piano in many pieces with orchestra: Rachmaninov's Piano Concerto no. 2; Beethoven's *Emperor* Concerto; Lambert's *The Rio Grande*.

Only 100 years after Cristofori made the earliest pianofortes, the piano had developed to become very like the instrument that we play today. This is a concert grand piano. There are smaller sizes and upright pianos, too.

The piano has a very wide pitch range.

Key facts

Instruments that use air to make sound are called aerophones.

Pipes

HAVE YOU EVER TRIED BLOWING across the top of an empty bottle? Or down a drinking straw? Try it–you should be able to make a sound. This is because when you blow into a hollow object the air inside starts to vibrate.

Wind instruments are basically hollow pipes with a part at one end called a mouthpiece. This is where the player blows into the pipe, making the air inside vibrate, which produces a musical note. In the same way that a short string produces a higher note than a long string (see pages 10–11), so the length of the pipe affects the pitch of the note. If you blow down a long pipe, it will sound a low note. A short pipe will sound a high note. Compare the length of the highest wind instrument in the orchestra, the piccolo, with one of the lowest, the double bassoon. The piccolo is only about 12 inches, but the double bassoon measures 6 yards! The great length of the double bassoon is folded four times in order to make the instrument easier to play.

Your own wind instrument

You have your own in-built wind instrument—your voice! You can make music by simply opening your mouth and singing. You can make sound because you have two pairs of membranes in your throat called your vocal cords. When air passes over your vocal cords, they vibrate, producing sound.

Woodwind and brass

In the orchestra wind instruments are divided into two sections, woodwind and brass. The woodwind section includes flutes and piccolos, oboes, clarinets, bassoons, and double bassoons. The brass section includes trumpets, French horns, trombones, and tubas. But the names woodwind and brass are misleading because although some "woodwind" instruments are made from wood, others are made from metal, and early "brass" instruments were made from wood, horn, bark, clay, and many other materials. As we shall see, the difference between the two sections lies mainly in the way that the instruments are played.

The actual size of the piccolo compared to part of the huge double bassoon.

Key facts

The pitch of a note made by a wind instrument depends upon the length of the column of vibrating air inside the pipe.

This instrument is from Chad, Africa. The fingerholes vary the pitch as they are covered and uncovered.

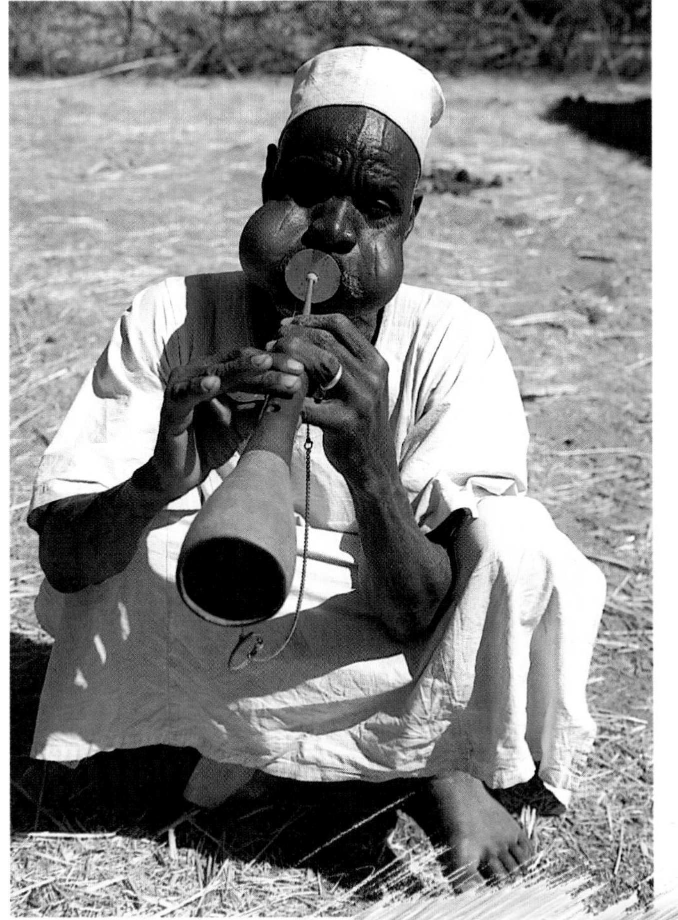

Pipes and flutes

The simplest wind instrument is a pipe with a mouthpiece at one end and holes cut down the length of the instrument. These holes are covered by the player's fingers and are called fingerholes. By opening and closing the holes, the player can alter the pitch of the note. When all the holes are covered, the instrument sounds its lowest note. If the bottom hole is uncovered, air escapes through the hole. This means that the length of the column of vibrating air is shorter, producing a higher note. Many different notes can be played on a single pipe by covering and uncovering the fingerholes.

Whistles and early flutes

Simple wind instruments formed from animal bones were made by some of the first human beings 20,000 years ago. These bone flutes produced whistling sounds. The native peoples of South America made clay whistles in the shapes of animals, birds, and people. Another early type of flute was made up of several pipes of different lengths joined together. These pipes were called panpipes. The panpipes are played by blowing across the top of each pipe (see page 24).

As different versions of the flute appeared all over the world, many different ways of playing the instrument also developed. Some

Krishna plays his side-blown flute to woo a beautiful woman.

were played by blowing straight down the pipe. Others, like the panpipes, were played by blowing across the top of the pipe. In Asia flute players held their instruments sideways, blowing across a hole in the side of the instrument (like the modern orchestral flute). There are many stories about the Indian Hindu god Krishna in which he plays the flute so beautifully that girls fall in love with him, and lost cattle make their way back to him. Perhaps the most unusual way of playing a flute is by blowing air through the nose. Nose-flutes are common in the Pacific islands of Polynesia and Micronesia.

The story of Pan

The panpipes get their name from the ancient Greek god Pan. Pan was in love with a young girl, but she was afraid of him and tried to run away. When the other gods saw that she could not escape, they changed her into a reed to protect her. Pan was so unhappy that he made an instrument from the reed and played upon it to console himself. This instrument became known as the panpipes.

Pan dares to challenge the god Apollo to a contest in music.

Recorders

In Europe in the 16th and 17th centuries, a kind of end-blown flute called the recorder was very popular. The recorder was made out of wood and had a soft, gentle sound. There were several different sizes of recorders, ranging from the tiny, high-pitched sopranino to the deep great bass. Music for the recorder was often written for a group, or consort, of different-sized recorders. But in the 17th century, the side-blown flute became more popular.

Theobald Boehm invented a system of hole-coverings, or keys, for the flute.

Side-blown flutes

Side-blown flutes made at this time had open holes that were covered by the player's fingers. Gradually flute makers added hole-coverings called keys to make the instrument easier to play. The most famous flute designer, Theobald Boehm (1794–1881), devised a system of keys to cover all the holes on the flute. Boehm's design has hardly been altered and is used to make the metal flutes played in orchestras and windbands today (see the photograph on page 81).

The flute and piccolo

The woodwind section sits in the center of the orchestra, with the flutes at the front. The piccolo is a small version of a flute that plays very high notes.

This is the flute's position in the orchestra.

This is the normal range of the flute.

LISTEN OUT FOR the flute in: Bach's Suite no. 2; Debussy's *Prélude à l'après-midi d'un faune* and the piccolo in Prokofiev 's *Lieutenant Kijé*.

Japanese musicians playing side-blown flutes. The flutes here are made from wood, while those used in the orchestra are usually made from metal.

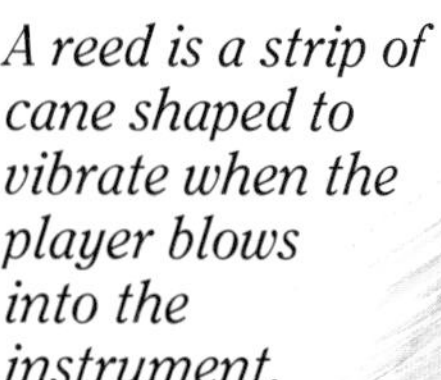

A reed is a strip of cane shaped to vibrate when the player blows into the instrument.

Reeds in pipes

Some wind instruments have a special kind of mouthpiece that contains one or two strips of cane (sometimes plastic). These strips of cane are called reeds. When the player blows into the instrument, the reed vibrates, making the air inside the instrument vibrate, too. The reed makes the sound of the instrument less clear and breathy than the sound of the flute.

Some reed instruments, such as the clarinet and the saxophone, have a single piece of cane in the mouthpiece. A type of clarinet was played in ancient Egypt 3,000 years ago. This was a double clarinet with two pipes joined side by side. Each pipe had a mouthpiece made out of a thin tube with a "tongue" cut out that acted as the reed–vibrating in the player's mouth. Both pipes had four to six fingerholes to play tunes. Other types of double clarinets are still found in many parts of the world, including the pungi, which is a favorite instrument of snake charmers in India.

A snake charmer plays a type of double clarinet to charm his snake!

The modern clarinet

The modern clarinet was the last of the main woodwind instruments to join the orchestra. It was invented some time around 1700 by a German instrument-maker called Johann Denner. But it was not until 1800 that the clarinet joined the orchestra. It was a clarinet-maker who invented the saxophone. Adolphe Sax was trying to make improvements to the clarinet, but in doing so he designed a new instrument–the saxophone–in the early 1840s. It was soon used in military bands in France (where Sax worked).

The saxophone is a very popular instrument today. It is often played by jazz musicians.

Double reeds

Many instruments have a mouthpiece made out of two pieces of cane, shaped and tied together. This is called a double reed. The canes vibrate against each other when the player blows into the mouthpiece, making a harsh, buzzing noise. The oboe and the bassoon both have double reeds. Instruments with double reeds are much older and more widely played than those with single reeds. One instrument from Sumer in the Middle East dates back about 4,800 years.

Bagpipes are played all over the world. This military bagpiper in Pakistan is performing on the Scottish Highland pipes.

Key facts

A drone is a continuous, unchanging note that is played at the same time as a melody. Many instruments have drones, including the bagpipes (see below).

The Indian shahnai

In India a double-reed instrument called a shahnai is still as important today as it was 1,000 years ago as an instrument to be played for dancing and in temples and mosques. The shahnai was also played at the gates of cities to welcome important visitors. In the 14th and 15th centuries, an instrument called a shawm became popular in Europe. This double-reed instrument had

Bagpipes

Bagpipes are reed instruments. You might have heard Scottish Highland bagpipes, but bagpipes are also played in Asia and Africa, as well as many other European countries. Bagpipe players blow air into a bag that is held under the arm. Air is then squeezed by the player's arm out through the pipes. The pipes have reeds inside them that vibrate as the air is forced out. Bagpipe players have to blow very hard to keep the bag full of air!

been introduced from the Middle East. Shawms made a loud buzzing sound and were played outdoors and to accompany dances. By the 16th century there were shawms in all sizes, including the great bass shawm, which was about 9.5 feet long!

The oboe

The shawm became less popular after the introduction of the oboe, which was developed from the treble shawm. The oboe was a more refined instrument than the shawm, with a less raucous noise. It quickly became popular with composers, such as the English composer Henry Purcell. In 1694, he wrote oboe solos into his piece *Come, Ye Sons of Art Away*. From the 18th century onward, the oboe was a regular member of the orchestra.

This early oboe has fingerholes that are covered and uncovered by the player's fingers. Modern oboes have keys.

Music at the Japanese court

The courtly music of Japan is called gagaku which means "elegant" or "correct" music. The gagaku orchestra includes wind, string, and percussion instruments. The melody of the gagaku music is played by a kind of shawm called a hichiriki and flutes. There is also an unusual wind instrument called a sho, which is a mouth organ with 17 pipes that can be used to play chords. The percussion section is made up of different-size drums and gongs, and the strings include kotos (see page 15) and a type of lute. The tradition of gagaku music has survived for over 1,000 years, and it is still heard today at the imperial palace in Japan.

The musicians at the front of the gagaku orchestra are playing flutes. At the back you can see two players blowing into mouth organs called shos.

The clarinet and bass clarinet

The bass clarinet is twice as long as the normal clarinet and plays lower notes.

LISTEN OUT FOR the clarinet in: Prokofiev's *Peter and the Wolf;* Mozart's Symphony no. 39 (3rd movement).

Playing the clarinet in an orchestra.

The saxophone

The saxophone combines certain elements of a brass and a woodwind instrument. It is made of metal, but it has a single reed in the mouthpiece and uses keys.

LISTEN OUT FOR the saxophone especially in jazz and pop music. The saxophone is sometimes played in the orchestra. You can hear it in: Mussorgsky's "The Old Castle" from *Pictures at an Exhibition* (orchestrated by Ravel).

This painting by the French artist Edgar Degas shows a bassoonist playing in an orchestra.

The bassoon and double bassoon

The double bassoon is sometimes called the contrabassoon. It plays the deepest notes in the woodwind section.

LISTEN OUT FOR the bassoon in: Stravinsky's *The Rite of Spring* (opening bars) and the bassoon and double bassoon in: Dukas's *The Sorcerer's Apprentice.*

The oboe and English horn

The English horn is a larger version of the oboe with a curved mouthpiece. It plays deeper notes than the oboe.

LISTEN OUT FOR the oboe in: Grieg's "Morning" from *Peer Gynt* (with the flute); Vaughan Williams's Oboe Concerto; and the English horn in: Dvořák's Ninth Symphony ("From the New World"), playing the tune in the 2nd movement.

The clarinet's range and position are shown in red; the oboe's are shown in blue; the English horn's in yellow; and the bassoon's in purple.

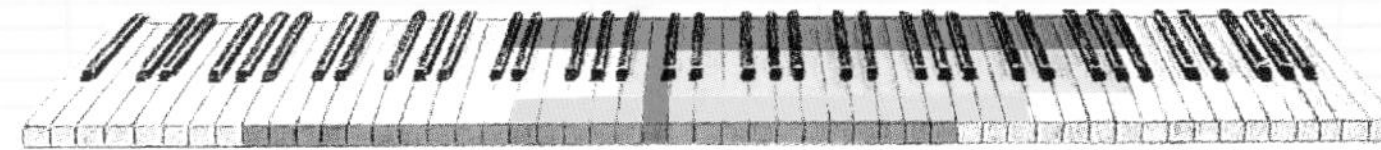

The organ

The organ was invented by the ancient Greeks over 2,000 years ago. The first organs used water power to push air through the pipes. Today electric fans do the same job. The biggest organs have thousands of pipes. The deepest notes on the organ are produced by pipes over 32 feet long.

The pipes of an organ in a church in Germany. The pipes vary in length and width to produce different pitches.

Trumpet calls

In 1923, the tomb of one of the ancient Egyptian pharaohs (kings), Tutankhamen, was opened up for the first time since his death, over 3,000 years ago. Inside, many rich treasures were found, including two trumpets. The trumpets were about 20 inches long. One was made of silver, the other of copper. They were probably used for playing fanfares on special occasions.

Roman trumpeters

Trumpets were also played by the ancient Greeks and Romans. In the Roman army, trumpets were very important signaling instruments. A long, straight trumpet called a tuba was used to accompany marching and to sound the attack and retreat. It was also sounded in the heat of a battle in order to frighten enemy soldiers with its raucous cry! Other Roman military trumpets included the lituus, which had a curled end in the shape of a "J," and a long, looped instrument in the shape of a "G" called a buccina. All these instruments made a loud, clear noise that could be easily heard a great distance away.

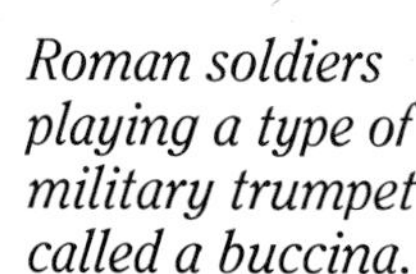

Roman soldiers playing a type of military trumpet called a buccina.

The modern trumpet has valves to produce different pitches.

Key facts

The sound of a "woodwind" instrument is produced by blowing across or down a hole in a pipe, sometimes using a reed.

The sound of a "brass" instrument is produced by vibrating the lips against a mouthpiece. This makes the air inside the instrument vibrate, too.

Modern trumpets

Today long, straight trumpets are still used to play ceremonial music for special occasions. But the trumpets played in bands and orchestras are folded up to make them easier to hold and play. The trumpet is a member of the brass section of the orchestra (see page 33), together with the trombone, tuba, and French horn. These instruments are usually made of brass or other metals, but there is a more important similarity between them. All these instruments have a cup-shaped mouthpiece. So the main difference between brass and woodwind instruments is not the material from which they are made: it is the way in which they are played. Modern brass instruments do not have holes and keys like the woodwind instruments. Instead they have valves (see page 87).

The Swiss Alphorn can be over 9 feet long.

Large trumpets

Simple trumpets are played all over the world. The native people of Australia, the Aborigines, play a type of wooden trumpet called a didgeridoo. This instrument is made out of a hollow tree branch, and it is usually about 51 inches long. The Swiss Alphorn can be up to 9 feet in length. The Alphorn is used by herders in the high Alpine valleys to send signals from one valley to another.

Many brass instruments are played in brass bands including trumpets, bugles, cornets, and larger instruments, such as euphoniums and sousaphones.

The trombone player pushes and pulls the slide in and out to produce different pitches.

Trombone slides

Some trombones have valves, but many trombonists play simple slide trombones. The design of these trombones has changed very little since the 1500s. A slide trombone has a U-shaped piece of tubing that moves in and out. As the player pushes the slide out, the tube becomes longer, and the trombone sounds deeper notes. As the player pulls the slide in, the tube becomes shorter, and the trombone sounds higher notes. Valve trombones have a slide, too, but the valves help to make the instrument easier to play. Trombones became regular members of the orchestra in the late 18th century. Early trombones were called sackbuts from the old French word *saqueboute,* which means "pull-push."

Hunting horns

The simplest kind of horn is a curved instrument, often made out of the horn of an animal. Horns can also be made from large shells, wood, elephant tusks, and metal. The sound is produced from all these different kinds of horns by the vibrations of the player's lips. Simple horns are still used in many parts of the world for sending signals and in religious ceremonies. In Europe, horns were used for sending signals while hunting. Hunting horns were usually made from metal, coiled into a round shape. The coil fitted over the hunter's shoulder, so that the horn could be easily carried on horseback. The orchestral French horn developed from these coiled hunting horns.

A detail from a 15th-century tapestry showing a man out hunting with his dogs. In his hand he is holding a hunting horn.

The trumpet

The brass section sits behind the woodwinds in the orchestra. The trumpets often sit behind the bassoons.

LISTEN OUT FOR the trumpet in many jazz pieces. In the orchestra you can hear it in: Handel's "The trumpet shall sound" from *Messiah;* Gershwin's *An American in Paris.*

The French horn developed from the hunting horn, which curled around the hunter's shoulder. Modern French horns have valves, which help the player to sound different pitches.

The French horn

The French horns sit next to the trumpets.

LISTEN OUT FOR the French horn in: Tchaikovsky's Fifth Symphony (2nd movement); Beethoven's *Eroica* Symphony (3rd movement); Prokofiev's *Peter and the Wolf* (three horns play the wolf).

Tubas are played in orchestras and brass bands as well as in jazz bands.

The trombone and tuba

The trombones and tuba often sit at the back of the orchestra behind the trumpets.

LISTEN OUT FOR the trombone in jazz music, and in: Mozart's "Tuba mirum" from *Requiem;* Dvořák's Eighth Symphony (last movement)

LISTEN OUT FOR the tuba in: Britten's *Young Person's Guide to the Orchestra*; Wagner's Overture to *The Mastersingers.*

The position and range of the trumpet are shown in red; the French horn's position and range are shown in blue; the trombone's are in yellow; and the tuba's in purple.

Percussion

PERCUSSION INSTRUMENTS MAKE A SOUND when they are hit or shaken. Some percussion instruments, such as glockenspiels and xylophones, sound pitched notes when they are struck. They are called tuned percussion. Other percussion instruments simply make interesting noises without sounding any particular pitch when they are struck or shaken. They are called untuned percussion.

Simple percussion

Many percussion instruments are very simple. Stamping tubes, for example, are hollow tubes often made out of bamboo, which are stamped against the ground. Different size and width sticks make sounds at different pitches. Scrapers have a notched edge, which makes a rasping noise when they are rubbed against a stick. Scrapers were made by the earliest peoples out of pieces of bone, shells, or even stones. In Portugal, two pine cones are rubbed together as scrapers.

Key facts

There are two groups of percussion instruments: idiophones sound when they are hit or shaken. Membranophones have a tightly stretched skin, which vibrates when it is hit.

Rattles

Rattles are found all over the world and are made out of almost any material. The simplest rattles are the dried seed heads of flowers, which contain rattling seeds. Some rattles have jingles attached, made out of metal discs. This type of rattle is called a sistrum. It was played in ancient Egypt, Greece, and Rome, and it is still played in religious services in churches in Ethiopia, Africa.

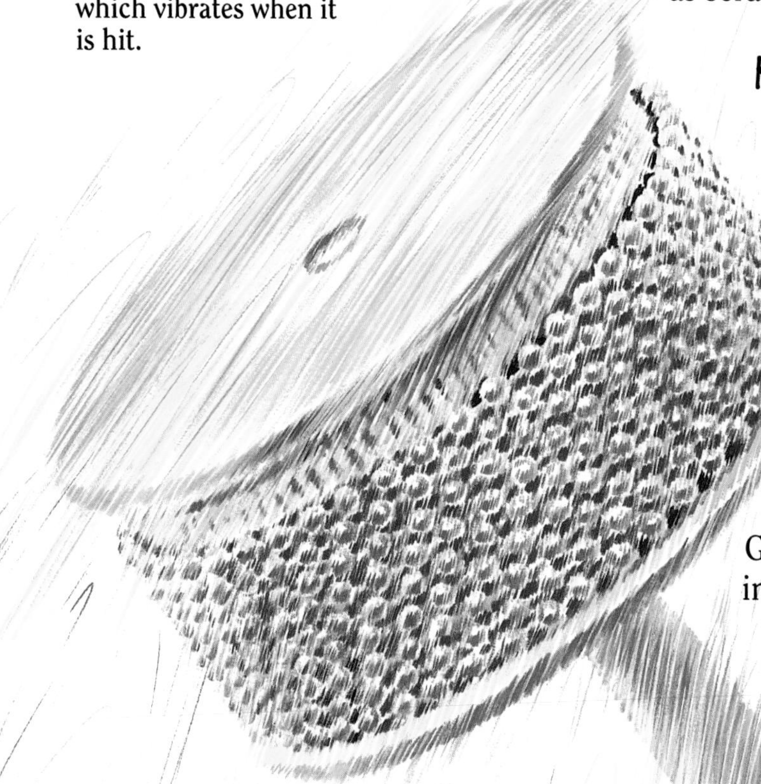

This rattle is called a cabaca and is from South America. It has steel beads strung around the outside, which move when the rattle is shaken.

Morris dancers attach bells to their legs. The bells jingle as they dance.

Jingles for dancing

Jingles are often made out of a string of small metal bells, which tinkle when they are shaken. Shells, nuts, and bits of animal bone are also used in different parts of the world to make jingles. Sometimes jingles are worn by dancers around the ankles or wrists. When the dancers move, the jingles tinkle and provide an accompaniment to the dancing.

Clashing and crashing

Cymbals and gongs both make a loud clashing noise when they are hit hard. In the orchestra two cymbals are often hit together to give a deafening crash at an exciting point in a piece of music. The gong, too, makes a huge noise, but it is usually hung on a stand and played with a large beater.

Cymbals

Cymbals are mentioned many times in the Bible. One line from the Psalms says, "Praise Him upon the loud cymbals; Praise him upon the high-sounding cymbals." The "loud cymbals" were probably wide and flat, rather like modern cymbals. The "high-sounding cymbals" were smaller, cup-shaped cymbals, which probably made a tinkling noise.

Today a suspended cymbal and "hi-hat" cymbals are often part of the drum kit (see page 41) used in jazz and pop music. The suspended cymbal is called a crash cymbal because it is often hit with a loud "crash." It is mounted on a metal stand and played with hard sticks or with a soft wire brush. "Hi-hat" cymbals are also mounted on a metal stand, but they can be clashed together by operating a foot lever.

A small boy holds a pair of child-sized cymbals. Orchestral cymbals are much bigger than these.

Gongs

Gongs are very important instruments in Asia–especially in the Far Eastern countries. Rich families had gongs as a sign of their wealth–owning a large gong showed that the family was very wealthy. Some gongs were known by names, such as "Sir Tiger." Gongs can be made to different thicknesses so that they play different pitches. In Thailand and Burma up to 24 tuned gongs are mounted in a circular wooden frame. This is called a gong chime. The player sits in the middle of the frame and plays the gong chime with beaters.

Gamelan orchestras

In Indonesia whole orchestras are made up of tuned gongs, as well as other percussion instruments such as

The gong is hung up and struck with a soft beater.

A gamelan orchestra from Bali in Indonesia. The barrel drums in the foreground set the speed of the music.

Steel drums

One unusual percussion instrument comes from the island of Trinidad in the Caribbean. It is the steel drum, made from a large oil drum. The oil drum is heated and hammered so that different parts of the top of the drum sound certain notes when hit with a beater. Steel bands have up to 100 performers, each playing two or three drums. Some drums have deeper notes than others. The steel drum that sounds the highest pitches is called a ping pong. Below that is the guitar pan and the cellopan, and the deepest drum is called the boom. Steel bands play all kinds of music, from the swinging rhythms of calypso to arrangements of music by classical composers.

A steel drum band. Different areas on top of the drum sound different notes when they are hit with a beater.

drums and metallophones (these are instruments like xylophones, but they have metal bars). These orchestras are called gamelans. A gamelan usually has between 12 and 20 players. The instruments of the gamelan are often beautifully decorated, with metallophones in the shapes of dragons or birds, and gongs hung from stands decorated with snakes and other animals. Gamelan music is arranged according to the pitches of the instruments. All the instruments play the same theme, but the highest-pitched instruments play it at a fast speed, the middle-pitched instruments at a medium speed, and the lowest instruments at a slow speed. Drum players set the speeds.

Korean bronze bells. Bells that are struck with a beater are very popular in the Far East.

Ringing and chiming

If you have ever heard church bells, you will know that bells sound notes with different pitches. The tunes rung by church bells are called peals. In England, church bells are often rung by groups of bell ringers. Each person plays one bell by pulling on a rope to make the bell swing up or down. As the bell swings, a metal tongue inside (called the clapper) hits the side of the bell and sounds a note. The bell ringer must pull the rope at exactly the right moment to make the bell sound correctly in the peal. This is called change ringing.

The oldest bell in the world is Chinese, and it is about 5,000 years old. Bells are very important in China and Japan, where they are used in temples for religious ceremonies. Temple bells do not usually have a clapper; instead they are sounded by being struck with a beater. Huge temple bells are used in Japanese temples to call people to prayer. These bells are so big that they are struck by swinging a wooden beam against the side of the bell. On New Year's Eve the sound of these temple bells marks the arrival of the New Year, as they are struck slowly from temples all over Japan.

Banging and beating

Drums come in all shapes and sizes and are played in all parts of the world. Drums are made from a hollow base with a skin stretched tightly over the top. When the skin is hit by the player, it vibrates, making the air inside the base vibrate, too. The base acts as a resonator (see page 11). There is one kind of drum that is made from a piece of solid wood and has no skin top. This is called a slit drum. Slit drums are made from wood or bamboo, which is hollowed out through a slit in the side. Slit drums are often carved

African long drums being played in Burundi. Long drums are usually made from hollowed-out tree trunks with animal skins stretched over one end.

into unusual shapes. In Japan a slit drum in the shape of a fish is played during religious ceremonies.

Drums are used for many different purposes. Throughout history drums have been played in battles. Sometimes drumbeats were played as signals to the soldiers to prepare to march or attack. At other times drums were used to make a loud din in order to terrify the enemy soldiers.

Japanese drums

In Japan special types of drums provide an accompaniment for the traditional Noh theater. Noh plays take place on a bare stage, and the

Slit drums are hollowed out of a solid piece of wood.

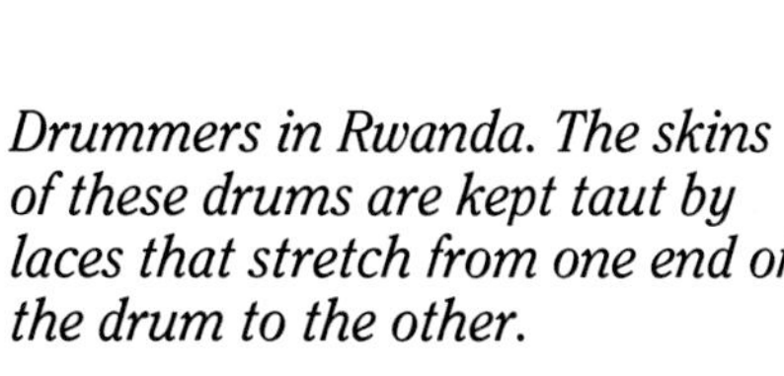

Drummers in Rwanda. The skins of these drums are kept taut by laces that stretch from one end of the drum to the other.

actors wear masks. They are accompanied by drums, a flute, and also a chorus. The main kind of Noh drum is called a kotsuzumi. It has a wooden body with a skin drum head at either end. The skins are held on by two ropes, one laced from one end to the other, and the other looped around the middle. The player holds the ropes with one hand. When the player squeezes the ropes with his hand, the drum skins become even more tightly stretched. Like the strings on a guitar or violin (see page 10), when the skins are stretched more tightly, the pitch of the note produced changes. The kotsuzumi player plays several different sounds including one that is called pon. Pon is played by squeezing the ropes hard at the exact moment that the fingers of the other hand hit the drum head. This produces a change of pitch.

The sound of juju

The talking drums are an important part of the juju groups from Nigeria in Africa. Juju mixes the sounds of the talking drums with electric guitars and percussion.The melodies and rhythms of juju are from African music, but a rock sound is added by the electric guitars.

Talking drums

In Africa a similar technique is used to play the talking drums. Talking drums are played in many parts of West Africa. One kind of talking drum is called a kalengo. It has a skin stretched over both ends, and it is an hourglass shape–narrower in the middle than at the ends. The skins are held in place by laces made from pieces of leather tied tightly from one end of the drum to the other. The laces are squeezed to produce different pitches. These different pitches make the music of the kalengo sound much like some African languages. This is why the kalengo is called the talking drum. The kalengo is only one of many different kinds of drums in Africa, where the drum is an important instrument.

A side drum player in an orchestra. Notice how he holds the sticks.

Orchestral drums

There are several different kinds of drums played in the orchestra. The bass drum makes a deep booming sound when it is hit. The tambourine is a type of drum with jingles attached around the edge, which rattle when the instrument is hit or shaken. The timpani are tuned drums. The timpani player, called a timpanist, can change the pitch of the notes sounded by the timpani by tightening or loosening the skin of each drum. This is usually done with a foot pedal, which is attached to the skin. The side drum has a completely different sound from the tuned timpani. This is because the side drum has several lengths of twisted wire (or sometimes other materials such as nylon) stretched inside the drum. This is called a snare, and the side drum is sometimes known as a snare drum. When the player hits the side drum, the snare vibrates inside the drum. This gives a very clear and brilliant sound. The side drum player has to learn how to play a roll. A roll is played by tapping the drum with the drumsticks so fast and so evenly that the listener cannot hear the individual beats. To learn to play a good roll takes many hours of hard practice.

The drum kit

In rock bands and jazz groups, the drummer often plays several instruments, all mounted together to form a drum kit. The drum kit is usually made up of a bass drum, a snare drum, "tom-tom" drums, a "hi-hat" cymbal, and a crash cymbal (see page 35) as well as another suspended cymbal called a "ride" cymbal. The bass drum lies on its side and is played by the player's foot pressing a foot pedal. The "tom-tom" drums are small drums that give a clear, high-pitched sound. The "ride" cymbal is tapped with a stick. Many other instruments can be added to the drum kit, depending upon the sounds the drummer wants to produce. These instruments often include gongs, bongos (a kind of small drum played with the hands), and even sometimes a tabla.

The Indian tabla

In India, the tabla is a vital instrument in music making. The full name of the tabla is the tabla-banya, because the tabla is actually two drums–the tabla played with the right hand, and the banya played with the left. The players vary the way their hands hit the tabla to produce the sound they want. In a group of instruments, the tabla sets the beat.

Timpani

There can be anything from two to six or more timpani in an orchestra. In Hector Berlioz's *Grande messe des morts* (Requiem) there are 16 timpani!

The timpani are tuned drums.

LISTEN OUT FOR the timpani in: Nielsen's Fourth Symphony; Berlioz's "Tuba mirum" from *Requiem*; Beethoven's Ninth Symphony and Richard Strauss's *Also sprach Zarathustra.*

The timpanist usually sits at the center back of the orchestra.

Playing tunes

Some orchestral percussion instruments can be used to play tunes. The xylophone and the glockenspiel both have bars that are hit with beaters. The bars of the xylophone are made from wood, those of the glockenspiel from metal. The bars are different lengths so that each bar sounds a different note. The bars are arranged in the same pattern as the notes on a piano keyboard. The glockenspiel has a bright, clear tone. The xylophone has a much quieter tone, so orchestral xylophones usually have hollow metal resonators (see page 11) underneath each bar, to make the sound louder.

Tubular bells

If you listen to Tchaikovsky's "1812" Overture, toward the end you will hear bell-like peals ringing out over the rest of the orchestra. This is the sound of the tubular bells. This instrument is made from a series of metal tubes hung in a

Tubular bells are used for bell effects in an orchestra.

A beautiful curved xylophone from Thailand.

A large xylophone (right) being played at a festival in Guatemala, Central America.

Shaping molten metal on an anvil to make a horseshoe. An anvil and a car horn (right) are just two of the unusual percussion instruments to make an appearance in the orchestra.

frame. The tubes are different lengths to sound different pitches. The player strikes the tubes with a hammer to make a loud, clear bell-like sound.

Unusual orchestral percussion

Some composers ask for odd instruments to be included in the percussion section. Car horns, chains, a blacksmith's anvil, mugs hung from strings, and even a typewriter all make an appearance in various pieces of music. One of the most impressive "extras" is the thunder sheet. This is a large metal sheet, often hung from a tall ladder. When it is shaken, it sounds just like thunder.

Orchestral percussion

Here are some examples of percussion instruments that are regularly found in the orchestra: bass drum, snare drum, cymbals, glockenspiel, xylophone, tubular bells, triangle, tambourine, gong, and castanets.

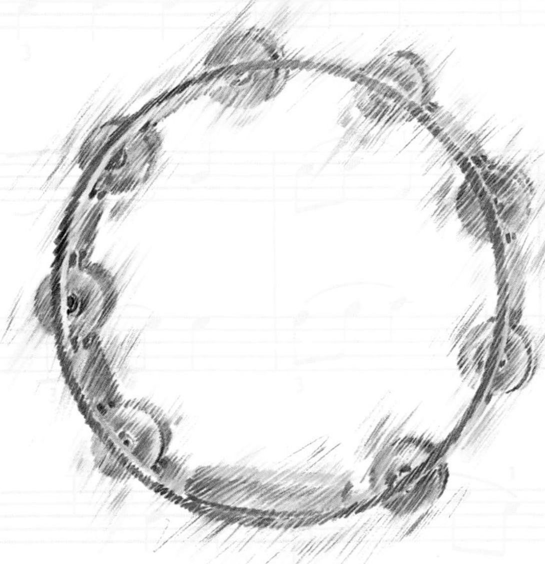

The glockenspiel, played here in a brass band, is also used in orchestral works. The tambourine (left) is shaken to produce a jingling sound.

LISTEN OUT FOR the percussion in: Tchaikovsky's "1812" Overture (tubular bells); Saint-Saëns's "Fossils" from *Carnival of the Animals* (xylophone); Ravel's *Bolero* (side drum); Bizet's *Carmen* (castanets); Liszt's Piano Concerto no. 1 (2nd movement) (triangle), and Tchaikovsky's Fourth Symphony (last movement) (cymbals).

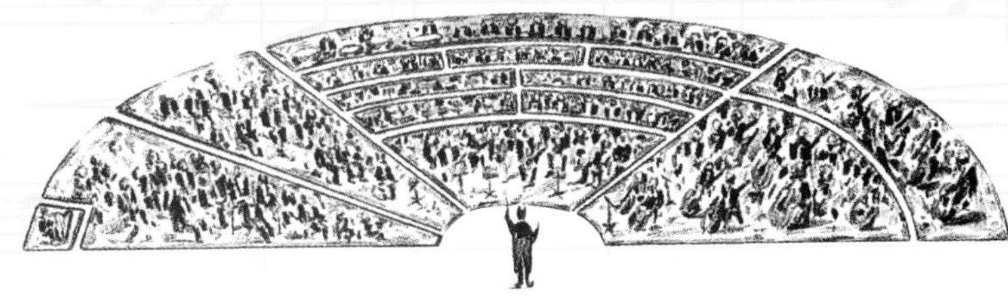

The percussion section is always at the back of the orchestra.

Electronic music

MANY INSTRUMENTS PLAYED IN POP and rock music today are electric instruments. The development of electronic music since the beginning of the 20th century has opened up a new world of sound. Individual instruments can produce louder sounds and a greater variety of sounds than ever before. Some composers and musicians create music in a recording studio that cannot be played "live" in a concert. Gradually, electronic music has become part of our everyday lives.

Two types of electronic music

There are two groups of electric instruments. The first group includes the most well-known electric instrument–the electric guitar–as well as the electric saxophone, violin, and flute. In these instruments the sound is still made by plucking a string or blowing down a pipe. But the sound is picked up electronically and made louder, or amplified, through a loudspeaker. The second group includes some of the earliest electric instruments to be invented, such as the telharmonium and the theremin. These instruments produce sound with electronic circuits. They make a weird, unearthly sound, completely unlike any other instrument. Included in this group are more up-to-date instruments such as the synthesizer and music generated by computers.

Key facts

Acoustic instruments are instruments in which the sound is produced by the vibrations made by, for example, plucking a string or blowing down a pipe. The sound is often amplified (made louder) by a hollow resonator. In electric instruments the sound is amplified or produced electronically.

Queen in concert. Brian May and John Deacon are both playing electric guitars.

An electric guitar.

The electric guitar

The electric guitar became popular during the 1950s, and today it is one of the most important instruments in pop and rock music. Many bands have two or three electric guitars, often a lead guitar, a rhythm guitar, and a bass guitar. The lead guitar plays tunes, and the other two provide accompaniment. Electric guitars often look quite different from acoustic guitars. This is because an acoustic guitar must have a hollow body that acts as a natural resonator (see page 11). But the sound of an electric guitar is amplified electrically, so there is no need for a hollow body. Most electric guitars have flat, solid bodies made from wood or plastic. The body of the electric guitar must be strong enough for the strings and electrical parts to be attached to it. But it can be any shape, and electric guitars are made in many unusual shapes.

How the guitar works

If you look at an electric guitar, you will see that underneath the strings is an oblong metal plate, with a small circular button positioned under each string. This is called the pickup (some guitars have more than one pickup). Each circular button on the pickup is actually a magnet. Underneath the magnets is a wire coil. When the strings of the guitar vibrate, the magnets produce an electric signal in the wire coil. Wire leads take the signal from the coil to a box called an amplifier and then to the loudspeaker. In the loudspeaker the signal is converted into the sounds that you hear. The amplifier makes the sound of the strings much louder than they would naturally be. Volume controls on the guitar and the amplifier allow the player to control exactly how loud or how soft the sounds are.

Music of the electric guitar

The electric guitar is played widely in rock and pop music, but some players have become famous for their use of the guitar, and its many different effects. Listen to the electric guitar playing of these famous performers: Eric Clapton, Jimi Hendrix, Frank Zappa, Pete Townsend (The Who), Brian May (Queen), Andy Summers (The Police), Robert Fripp, and Steve Vai.

The vibraphone.

Microphones

The electric violin has a pickup, like the electric guitar, as well as a volume control. The electric flute and saxophone both have small microphones inside the instrument, attached to amplifiers. The microphone picks up the air vibrations inside the instrument and sends them as electric signals to the amplifier. The signals are increased in the amplifier before going to the loudspeaker, where they are turned once again into sound.

The vibraphone

There is one orchestral instrument that uses an electric motor to create its unusual sound. This is the vibraphone. Its top looks like a glockenspiel, with metal bars arranged like the keys of the piano. But underneath the bars lie metal tubes that act as resonators. At the top of each tube is a small propeller, like the propeller on a plane. The propeller is driven by an electric motor, and it gives the vibraphone an unusual vibrating sound. You can hear the sound of the vibraphone in Britten's opera *A Midsummer Night's Dream* and Milhaud's Concerto for Marimba and Vibraphone.

Electronic sounds

The first instrument to produce electronic sounds was the telharmonium, invented in 1906. This machine was huge–it weighed 220 tons and was 59 feet long. Smaller and more successful electronic instruments were developed in the 1920s and 1930s. These included the theremin and the ondes martenot. The theremin was named after its inventor, Leo Theremin. It was also an unusual looking instrument, being a box with a metal rod sticking through the top and a metal loop out of one side. The electronic sound it produced was controlled by the distance of the player's hands from the rod

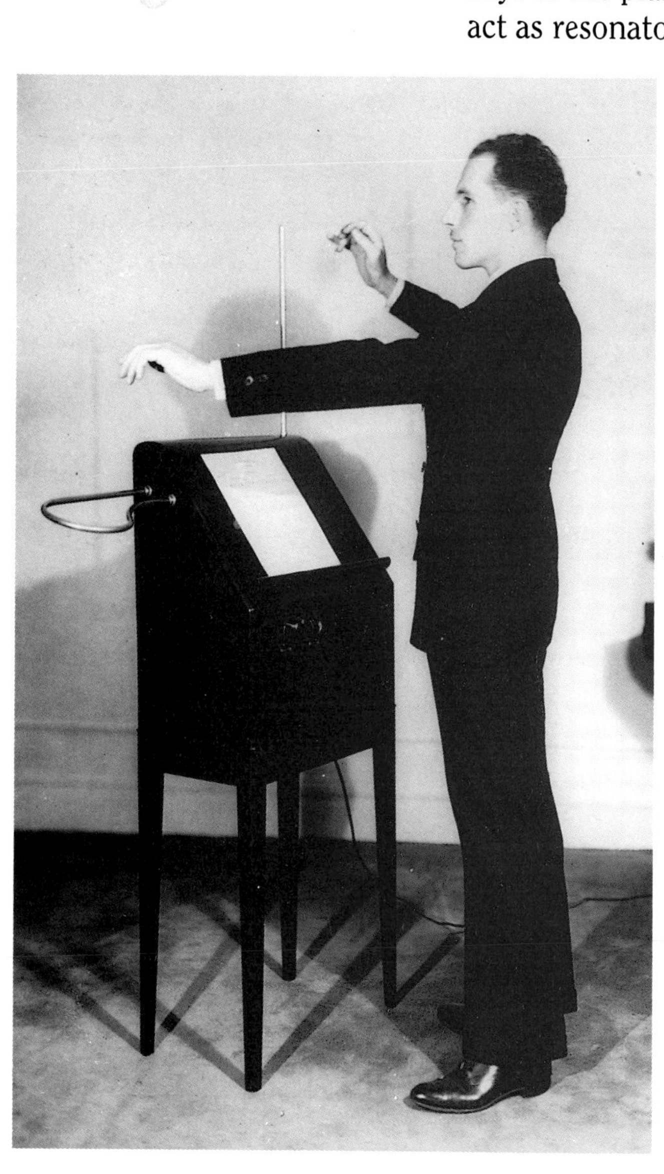

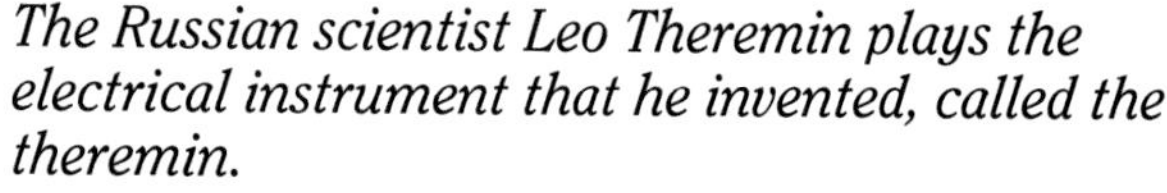

The Russian scientist Leo Theremin plays the electrical instrument that he invented, called the theremin.

and the loop. The player changed the pitch of the note by moving the right hand toward or away from the rod. The volume was controlled by how far the player's left hand was held from the loop. You can hear the strange sounds of the theremin on the recording of the song "Good Vibrations" by the Beach Boys.

The ondes martenot

The ondes martenot looks more familiar than the theremin, having a keyboard. It makes exotic, swooping sounds and is the only one of these early electronic instruments still played in orchestras today, for example in the *Turangalîla* Symphony by the French composer Olivier Messiaen (see page 67).

Drum pad and synthesizer

Some modern electronic instruments reproduce the sounds of traditional acoustic instruments. The drum pad, for example, is a thin plastic pad with pickups underneath that sense how hard the drummer hits the pad. Hitting the pad with a stick produces an electronic signal that gives a drum sound. The synthesizer, too, can reproduce the sounds of almost every instrument in the orchestra. But the synthesizer not only produces many other sounds, it also allows the musician to work with sound in completely new ways.

Playing a synthesizer. Synthesizers can store sounds and series of notes.

Working with sounds

Many synthesizers can "sample" sounds. For example, you can sing a single note into a microphone on the synthesizer. The synthesizer will analyse, or "sample," the sound of that single note. You can then use the sampled sound to play any note on the synthesizer. You can store your sampled sounds in the synthesizer and build up your own collection. Sequencers in a synthesizer are small computers that memorize sound. If you play a group of notes on the synthesizer, the sequencer will memorize them. The sequencer will then play this musical phrase back, as many times as you want. Some sequencers can remember several musical phrases and will play them back in any order you want. The use of a phrase of music that is repeated over and over again is called ostinato (see page 68). Many pop musicians use sequencers to make backing tracks.

A drum machine produces drum sounds electronically.

Drum machines

Some bands have done away with a drummer altogether and use a drum machine instead. A drum machine either produces a drumlike sound electronically, or uses "sampled" drum sounds from real drums. Drum machines are used especially in disco and funk music, where a precise, unchanging beat is needed. Once a rhythm pattern has been fed into the machine, a sequencer memorizes the pattern and repeats it. Some drum machines have various common rhythm patterns already set and memorized. All the player needs to do is to set the machine to the right pattern and off it goes!

Sound produced by the singer in the studio is controlled by technicians working at the mixing desk (foreground).

Electronic music

Many musicians have experimented with the new possibilities provided by developments in electronic instruments and computers. Some musicians have experimented with sounds recorded on tape machines, producing new and strange effects by speeding up and slowing down the sounds, recording one sound on top of another, and playing sounds in reverse. This kind of music is called *musique concrète*. The German composer Karlheinz Stockhausen has written a *musique concrète* piece using recordings of one boy singing and speaking. Stockhausen has altered the

MIDI

MIDI stands for Musical Instrument Digital Interface. MIDI is a computer language that allows synthesizers and sequencers made by different manufacturers to work together. With MIDI leads, you can connect up your computer, synthesizer, electric guitar, and sampler and you're off!

recordings to create a new piece, with the effect of many voices singing and speaking.

Computer-programmed music

Other musicians use computer programs to create musical sounds. One piece by Lejaren Hiller and John Cage uses seven harpsichords and 51 tapes of computer sounds. The seven performers switch on the tapes and play the harpsichord parts in any order they wish. So the overall sound of the piece is left to chance and will sound different at every performance.

Today, electronic music is a familiar sound to us–even if we sometimes don't realize that it is electronic music! For example, the sound tracks and sound effects for films and television programs are often created on synthesizers and computers. In Paris an institute of electronic music (called IRCAM) opened in 1978. At the institute musicians and composers such as Pierre Boulez and Luciano Berio work and experiment with all kinds of computer music.

Electronic rock

Many pop and rock musicians use the most up-to-date electronic equipment for recording and for their live shows. But some musicians have become particularly well-known for their experiments with electronic music. You could try listening to electronic music by any of these musicians: Jean-Michel Jarre, Brian Eno, David Byrne, and Peter Gabriel.

Using synthesizers and other electronic equipment, Jean-Michel Jarre performs spectacular concerts in front of huge crowds.

Medieval and Renaissance music

Music		History
	1100	12th century
Period of troubadours and trouvères		
	1200	13th century
Period of early polyphony		Magna Carta in England (1215)
Sumer is icumen in written down about 1260		Marco Polo travels to China (1275–93)
	1300	14th century
		Hundred Years' War between France and England begins (1337)
		Black Death in Europe (1347–50)
Machaut *Mass de Notre Dame* (1360)		
	1400	15th century
Dufay Mass *Se la face ay pale* (1440s)		Beginning of the period called the Renaissance
		Gutenberg invents printing (1454)
Early music printing (1476)		Columbus sails to America (1492)
Josquin Desprez first book of Mass settings printed (1502)	1500	16th century
First Italian madrigals		Luther attacks Roman Catholic Church (1517)
Palestrina first book of Masses (1554)		Magellan's fleet circumnavigates the world (1519–22)
Byrd member of Chapel Royal at court of Queen Elizabeth I		Reformation in Europe
Musica transalpina published in England (1588)		Spanish Armada defeated (1588)
	1600	17th century
Period of English madrigal		

THE HISTORY OF WESTERN MUSIC is short when compared to the musical traditions of India, Africa, China, and Japan. Western music has its origins in the music of the ancient Greeks and Romans. But we know little about the kinds of music that were sung and played until music began to be written down.

As in many religions, music was an important part of worship in the Christian Church. When Gregory I was pope (A.D. 590–604), music sung in the mass started to be collected and written down. The music was a simple kind of melody, called plainsong (or plainchant). Plainsong is still sung in churches all over the world today. It is also known as "Gregorian chant," after Pope Gregory.

Pope Gregory I

Key facts

The mass is the central ceremony of the Roman Catholic Church. The words of some parts of the mass change; other parts always stay the same. The five sections that stay the same are called the Kyrie, Gloria, Credo, Sanctus, and Agnus Dei. These are the parts that were set to music by composers such as Dufay, Josquin Desprez, Palestrina, and Byrd.

Musicians provide entertainment at the house of a French nobleman.

Traveling minstrels

Churches were not the only places where music could be heard in medieval Europe. Minstrels traveled around the courts of Europe, singing songs about love and heroic deeds. In France these minstrels were often noblemen, and they were known as troubadours or trouvères. As the minstrels sang, they accompanied themselves on the harp or lyre. Many of the minstrels' songs were written down in collections, some of which still survive today.

Music in many parts

Today we are used to hearing music that has a tune that is sung or played and an accompaniment, providing harmony, beneath. But the earliest plainsong had no accompaniment–it was a kind of wandering melody sung on its own. Gradually musicians began to write music in more than one part. Sometimes one voice would sing the melody, and another voice would sing a long note or drone (see page 27) beneath. This idea developed until composers were writing music with four or five different parts, all being sung at the same time. Music with more than one part is called polyphony, from the Greek words *poly* meaning "many" and *phone* meaning "sound" or "voice."

A group of church singers, or choristers, singing music that is written in many parts.

The importance of printing

An early printing press of 1520. Printing enabled people to preserve their words and music and allowed others to enjoy them.

Printing was invented in the West by a German, Johannes Gutenberg, in the middle of the 15th century (the Chinese had invented printing around A.D. 700). Music printing began about 1476. Before this time, music had to be copied out by hand, which took a long time and was very expensive. But printing meant that many copies of a piece of music could be made quickly and cheaply.

The madrigal

One of the most popular forms of music in the 16th century was the madrigal. A madrigal is a polyphonic piece set to poetry, usually with four or five parts sung by different voices. The first madrigal composers worked in Italy. Printed copies of their music soon spread the popularity of the madrigal across Europe. In 1588 a collection of Italian madrigals with their words translated into English was published in England. It was called *Musica transalpina,* "Music from across the Alps." This collection inspired many English composers to write madrigals, too.

One of the features of the madrigal was that composers used the music to illustrate what was happening in the

The oldest popular song

One of the oldest surviving popular songs was written down about 1260. The song is called *Sumer* [summer] *is icumen* [coming] *in*. It was sung in a round–with one part coming in after another. It is still sung today.

Three 16th-century musicians: a singer, a flautist, and a lute player.

Key facts

The term Renaissance is used to describe the period from roughly 1450 to 1600. The word *renaissance* means "rebirth." It marks a period in European history when there was a revival in art, literature, music, and learning.

words. For example, in the madrigal *As Vesta was from Latmos hill descending*, Thomas Weelkes sets the words "came running down amain" to descending patterns of notes. A sad madrigal by John Bennet starts with the words "Weep, O mine eyes" on long, held notes. Illustrating the words through the music in this way is called "word-painting."

Composing music for the Church

At the beginning of the 16th century, the Roman Catholic Church was the main religion in Europe. But in 1517, a German monk called Martin Luther nailed 95 "theses" or complaints to the doors of the church in Wittenberg in protest at corruption in the Church. He demanded reform, and he helped to start the change that is now called the Reformation.

During the Reformation many people broke away from the Catholic Church and set up their own churches. They were often called Protestants because they protested against the Roman Catholic Church. Luther wanted the congregation to take part in church services. In the Roman Catholic Church, plainsong

In 1517, Martin Luther nailed a list of 95 complaints about the Catholic Church to the doors of the church in Wittenberg. He helped to start the change that is now known as the Reformation.

Queen Elizabeth I dancing with the Earl of Leicester to the sounds of the court musicians.

was sung by the monks and in Latin–a language that most ordinary people did not understand. Luther collected together tunes that people could easily learn, set to words in their own language. These pieces are called chorales. Sometimes Luther composed the tunes for these chorales himself.

Byrd and Palestrina

Two great composers of the Renaissance, William Byrd and Giovanni Pierluigi da Palestrina, both wrote music for the Roman Catholic Church. Byrd was a Roman Catholic in England during the reign of Queen Elizabeth I. Elizabeth was a Protestant, but she did not persecute Byrd for his religion, and even employed him as a musician in the Chapel Royal. Byrd wrote music for three settings of the Roman Catholic mass, as well as music for the Anglican (the English Protestant Church) services. Byrd's mass settings were published in England, but without a title page so that the dangerous word *mass* did not appear. They were called "Kyries" instead. Byrd's masses may have been performed secretly at the homes of his Catholic friends. Palestrina, on the other hand, lived all of his life in Rome, the center of the Catholic Church. He wrote 105 settings of the mass, many dedicated to the pope.

TENOR
CANTIONES, QVAE AB
ARGVMENTO SACRAE VOCANTVR,
QVINQVE ET SEX PARTIVM, AVTORIBVS
Thoma Tallisio & Guilielmo Birdo Anglis, Serenissimæ Reginæ Maiestati à priuato Sacello generosis, & Organistis.
CVM PRIVILEGIO.
Excudebat Thomas Vautrollerius typographus Londinensis in claustro vulgo Blackfriers commorans,
1575.

William Byrd worked closely with another composer, Thomas Tallis, at the Chapel Royal. This is the title page to a set of pieces called Cantiones *that they published jointly in 1575.*

Baroque and Classical music

Music		History
First opera performed (1600)	1600 — 17th century	Beginning of the Baroque period
Monteverdi's opera *Orfeo* performed (1607)		Gunpowder Plot to overthrow James I of England (1605)
First public opera house opens in Venice (1637)		Pilgrim Fathers sail to North America (1620)
Monteverdi's opera *Return of Ulysses* (1641) performed in Venice		Louis XIV becomes King of France (1643)
		Charles I beheaded in England (1649)
Lully at court of Louis XIV		Isaac Newton and the theory of gravity (1687)
Stradivari making violins in Cremona	1700 — 18th century	
First piano built (1709)		George I of England crowned (Handel's patron) (1714)
Bach *Brandenburg* Concertos (1721)		Frederick the Great, King of Prussia crowned (flute player and musical patron) (1740)
First performance of Bach's *St. Matthew Passion*		
Haydn *Farewell* Symphony (1772)		Beginning of the Classical period
(1786–91) Mozart writes four great operas: *Marriage of Figaro, Don Giovanni, Cosi fan Tutte, The Magic Flute*		American Declaration of Independence (1776)
		French Revolution (1789)
	1800 — 19th century	
Beethoven's *Eroica* Symphony (1803)		Napoleon declares himself Emperor of France (1804)

For the composers of the 17th century, writing expressive music to illustrate words became very important. Composers now began to write music for a solo line with an accompaniment beneath. They also began to write music for specific instruments or voices.

The first opera

Opera began at the end of the 16th century. A group of poets and musicians in Florence, Italy, developed the idea of a dramatic work in which all the words are sung in a very expressive way. In 1607, an opera by Claudio Monteverdi was performed in Mantua, also in Italy. This opera was called *Orfeo*, and it is still performed today. The opera tells the story of Orpheus and Eurydice (see page 12).

A view of Florence in the 16th century.

George Frideric Handel sits with a score of his oratorio Messiah on a table in front of him.

The oratorio

Just as composers were writing new, expressive music for the opera house, so they also began to write dramatic music based on religious stories. An oratorio is rather like an opera that tells a story from the Bible, with soloists representing the different characters, a chorus, and orchestral accompaniment. The difference is that the singers in an oratorio do not usually wear special costumes or move around the stage. Probably the most famous of all oratorios is *Messiah* by G. F. Handel. *Messiah* tells the story of the birth and death of Jesus Christ.

Music at court

In European courts musical entertainments were often expensive occasions. The lavishness of these musical occasions was one way of showing the world how rich and important the ruler of the court was. In the 17th century in France, King Louis XIV employed several orchestras and choirs to

The sumptuous court of Louis XIV at Versailles. Louis XIV employed large numbers of musicians to entertain him.

Key facts

The word "Baroque" is often used to describe the art and music of the period from roughly 1600 to 1750. The word "Classical" is used to describe the music of the period from roughly 1750 to 1827 (the year of Beethoven's death).

Key facts

The system of rich families paying for the services of composers and musicians is called patronage.

The crucifixion of Christ. Passion oratorios relate the events leading up to and after Christ's crucifixion.

play and sing music for different courtly occasions. These included a group of 25 violins to play during the king's dinner; another different group of 24 violins to accompany him when he went to his country houses, and to play for balls; a choir for his private chapel; and a band of wind and brass players for ceremonial music and to accompany outdoor pageants.

Bach and the Passion

One type of oratorio became particularly popular in the Baroque period. Passion oratorios told the story of the events leading up to and just after Christ's crucifixion. Several composers wrote Passions, but the best examples are those written by J.S. Bach. From 1723, Bach worked in Leipzig, Germany, and one of the first of his compositions to be performed there was the *St. John Passion*. For this setting of the Passion story, Bach used words from St. John's Gospel in the Bible, as well as some other Passion poetry.

A few years later he wrote another setting using words from the Gospel of St. Matthew. Bach's Passions have a storyteller, called the Evangelist, who relates the events of the Passion. The story is broken up by choruses, solo songs called arias, and settings of chorales (see page 54). Often the chorus helps to tell the story, taking the part of the disciples at one point, and the part of the mob calling for Jesus's death at another. Bach uses the chorales and the arias to comment on the events of the story.

Church and Court

Before the 18th century, in order to earn a living musicians either had to find employment as church organists, or at court. J.S. Bach worked in the German city of Leipzig at the school attached to St. Thomas's Church. He composed music for Sunday services, trained the choir, and taught music in the school. Joseph Haydn, however, worked for nearly 25 years at the court of the Hungarian Prince Esterházy. He wrote music for the court orchestra to perform, and presented himself every day to the Prince to see if he wanted music played to him.

Joseph Haydn worked at the court of Prince Esterházy in Hungary for much of his life.

Haydn's farewell

Joseph Haydn was employed by Prince Esterhazy as his court musician in Vienna, and in the Esterhazy's summer palace outside the city. Although Haydn was treated well, he was still a servant who wore the livery (uniform) of the Prince's court. However, Haydn was a loyal and tactful servant.

When the Prince suddenly cancelled the court orchestra's summer holiday, Haydn wrote a new symphony called the 'Farewell'. It ended as each section of the orchestra in turn blew out their candles and walked out of the concert hall. Eventually only two violins remained. The Prince took the hint, and gave the musicians their holiday!

The symphony

One of the main types of orchestral music from the Classical period onward has been the symphony. A symphony usually has three or four parts, called movements. The movements of a Classical symphony have contrasting speeds, fast and slow, to give a well-ordered and balanced effect. Haydn wrote more than 100 symphonies, and Mozart about 50. Beethoven developed the symphony, even introducing a chorus and solo voices into his last symphony (number 9).

The beginning of public concerts

Up to the 17th century, composers were employed by the church or by wealthy patrons to write music. But during the 18th century, public concerts began, in which ordinary people would pay to come and hear an orchestra play a symphony, or to see an opera. Concert halls and opera houses opened all across Europe, and popular interest in music increased. This change meant that composers and musicians no longer had to rely entirely on the church or the court to make their livings.

The Vienna State opera house, which holds performances for the general public, was built in the 19th century.

The child prodigy Wolfgang Amadeus Mozart, pictured here at the keyboard accompanying his father and sister.

Mozart and his sister

Even as a young child, Wolfgang Amadeus Mozart showed his love of music. He and his sister, Marianne, both learned at a very early age how to play the harpsichord and to compose. When Wolfgang was only six years old, their father took his children on a tour of European courts. Wolfgang and Marianne played solos and duets to the courtiers. Marianne grew up to become a teacher and died in poverty in 1820. Wolfgang went on to compose some of the most famous symphonies and operas ever written. But he, too, died poor, in 1791.

Beethoven and Napoleon

In 1789 the people of France overthrew their king at the beginning of the French Revolution. These changes greatly influenced the composer Ludwig van Beethoven. The slogan of the French Revolution was "Liberty, Equality, Brotherhood," ideas that Beethoven thoroughly agreed with. When Napoleon Bonaparte took control of the country, Beethoven thought he was a hero and called his Third Symphony *Bonaparte*. But in 1804, when Napoleon declared himself Emperor of France, Beethoven felt that Napoleon was no longer acting like a revolutionary. He angrily tore out the title page with the name *Bonaparte* on it and called the symphony the *Eroica* (the "heroic symphony") instead.

Ludwig van Beethoven (above), like many other musicians, writers, and artists, was greatly influenced by the events of the French Revolution in 1789 (right).

Romantic music

Music	History
	1800 — 19th century
Beethoven *Pastoral* Symphony (1808)	
Schubert writes earliest songs (1811) Schubert *Erl-king* (1815)	First steamship crosses Atlantic (1819)
Berlioz *Fantastic Symphony* (1829)	
Mendelssohn *Hebrides Overture* (1832) Chopin piano pieces: études and mazurkas (1832) Liszt writing and performing piano music	Slavery abolished in British Empire (1833) Experiments with electric lighting (1848)
Adolphe Sax invents saxophone (early 1840s)	Gold Rush in America (1848)
Covent Garden opera house, London, opens (1858) J. Strauss "Waltz King" in Vienna	American Civil War (1861–65)
Smetana opera *The Bartered Bride* first performed (1866)	Suez Canal opens (1869)
Grieg *Peer Gynt* suite (1876) Dvořák Slavonic Dances for orchestra (1878) Clara Schumann performs at Philharmonic concerts in London	Telephone invented by Bell (1876) Phonograph (early gramophone) invented by Edison (1877)
Metropolitan Opera opens, New York (1883)	
Sibelius *Finlandia* (1899)	Statue of Liberty erected in New York (1886)
	1900 — 20th century
Elgar *Pomp and Circumstance* March no. 1 (1902)	

MANY COMPOSERS OF THE 19th century became particularly concerned with expressing emotions and moods through their music.

Romantic artists and musicians were often inspired by nature, and especially by the idea of a hero struggling against wild, untamed nature. We saw that Beethoven named his Third Symphony the *Eroica*, and Beethoven's music marks the turning point between the orderliness of Classical music and the freedom and passion of Romantic music.

Mood music

Many Romantic composers wrote instrumental music that tried to describe a scene, set a mood, or even tell a story. This kind of music became known as program music. When Mendelssohn visited the islands off the west coast of Scotland, he was particularly impressed by the wild scenery. He

The wild and beautiful scenery in Scotland inspired Mendelssohn to write an overture called The Hebrides.

Felix Mendelssohn.

wrote an overture (a short orchestral piece) called *The Hebrides* (also known as "Fingal's Cave"), which painted a picture of the Scottish landscape through music.

Berlioz took the idea further when he wrote his *Fantastic Symphony*. He gave the symphony an extra title, "Episode in the Life of an Artist," and the story behind the symphony was based on his own life. Berlioz was madly in love with an actress at the time, and through the music Berlioz describes his passion for her. He even imagines in one movement that he has killed her and is being led to the scaffold for execution.

Music for the piano

If one instrument is especially associated with the Romantic composers, it is the piano. By the 1840s the modern piano had developed–in fact there were now two types of pianos, the powerful concert grand (see page 21) and the smaller upright piano. Concert grands were played in concert halls, and uprights were found in drawing rooms all over Europe where they were used for family music-making.

The virtuoso Franz Liszt was an amazing pianist. This cartoon shows what people thought he was capable of!

Key facts

The term "Romantic" is used to describe art, music, and literature of the 19th century.

Composers such as Chopin and Liszt not only wrote music for the piano, but they were also talented players. Liszt, especially, delighted and amazed audiences all over Europe by his virtuosity. He wrote much piano music, including complicated reworkings of orchestral pieces to be played on the piano. One of the pieces Liszt rewrote for the piano was Berlioz's *Fantastic Symphony*.

Chopin plays the piano for an enthralled audience in 1829.

Women composers

"A woman must not desire to compose"–so wrote Clara Schumann in her diary in 1839. Clara Schumann was a talented virtuoso pianist who appeared in concerts all over Europe. She did compose music, mainly for the piano, but knowing that serious composition was not an accepted job for a woman, she devoted most of her energies to performing and to her family. Another talented musician, Fanny Mendelssohn, was sister to the more famous composer, Felix. Both children were trained in music, and Fanny advised her brother throughout his career about his musical compositions. She wrote some music of her own, but there was little opportunity for her to perform it. Although she was a talented pianist, her family allowed her to play only once in public, when she performed one of Felix's piano pieces.

Clara Schumann was a talented concert pianist, and a composer.

During the Romantic era a lot of music was written for smaller groups of musicians, such as the string quartet. The quartet is made up of two violinists, a viola player, and a cellist.

Chamber music

Music written for small groups of instruments is often known as chamber music. The most usual chamber music groups in the Classical period were string quartets (two violins, one viola, and a cello), and string trios (violin, viola, and cello). Haydn wrote about 70 string quartets and Mozart 26. In the Romantic period composers continued to write for string quartets, as well as music for other combinations of instruments. For example, Schubert's *Trout* Quintet is for violin, viola, cello, double bass, and piano, and his Octet (eight instruments) is for clarinet, French horn, bassoon, two violins, viola, cello, and double bass.

Schubert's songs

In his short life (he died when he was only 31), Schubert wrote over 600 songs, as well as operas, symphonies, and chamber music. Many of the songs are about love; others tell dramatic stories. One of the most exciting of Schubert's songs is called *The Erl-king*. It tells the story of a father carrying his young son on horseback through a wood. They are riding frantically "through night and storm" in order to escape from the wicked erl-king (king of the goblins). Eventually the erl-king appears in front of the child and kills him. The noise of the horse's hooves is heard in the pounding notes on the piano, which stop suddenly and dramatically as the boy dies at the end. Other Romantic song writers included Robert Schumann, Johannes Brahms, and later in the century, Hugo Wolf.

An evening of Schubert's music at the house of Joseph Spaun in 1868.

Dancing music

In coffeehouses, ballrooms, and salons in 19th-century Europe, everyone wanted to dance the waltz. It originally came from a German and Austrian folk dance called a ländler. But it was taken up by fashionable society in the 19th century and became very popular. Many composers wrote music for people to waltz to, but the most famous waltz-composer was Johann Strauss, who was called the "Waltz King" in his home city, Vienna.

Dancing the waltz at a court ball in 19th-century Vienna.

Nationalism in music

During the 19th century, people in many European countries became more aware of their national identity and traditions. Many composers reflected this new interest in nationalism by looking back to the folk music of their country. In Russia composers such as Nikolai Rimsky-Korsakov made use of Russian folk tunes in their music and based their operas on Russian history. In Czechoslovakia, Bedřich Smetena, Antonin Dvořák and Leoš Janáček all chose nationalist subjects for their operas and program music (see page 60). Other nationalist composers included Edvard Grieg in Norway, Jean Sibelius in Finland, and in England–Edward Elgar.

The Norwegian composer Edvard Grieg.

The orchestra

The size of the orchestra grew rapidly during the 19th century. At the end of the 18th century, Haydn and Mozart were writing symphonies for orchestras of about ten different instruments, with a total of about 47 players. At the end of the 19th century, the score of *Don Juan* by Richard Strauss calls for 21 different instruments, with a total of about 99 players.

The orchestra of the 18th century was usually directed by the lead violinist. As the orchestra grew and the music became more complicated, it became too difficult to play and control the orchestra. So the role of the conductor developed.

The conductor of an orchestra was, at one time, also the leading violinist.

The modern age

Music	History
Puccini opera *La Bohème* (1896)	Paris Exhibition and Eiffel Tower built (1889)
Elgar oratorio *The Dream of Gerontius* (1900)	1900 — 20th century
Scott Joplin *The Entertainer* and *Elite Syncopations* (1902) Debussy *La mer* (1905)	Model "T" Ford car produced (1908)
Mahler Eighth Symphony first performance (1910) Richard Strauss opera *Der Rosenkavalier* (1911) Stravinsky *The Rite of Spring* (1913)	Amundsen reaches South Pole (1911) *Titanic* sinks (1912) Panama Canal opens (1914) World War I (1914–18)
Louis Armstrong makes jazz recordings with *Hot Five* Gershwin *Rhapsody in Blue* (1924) Copland Piano Concerto (1926)	First films with sound (1927)
Prokofiev *Peter and the Wolf* (1936)	Hitler becomes Chancellor of Germany (1933)
Messiaen's *Turangalîla* Symphony (1948) First electronic music studio built (1951) Messiaen *Réveil des oiseaux (The waking of the birds)* piano and orchestra (1953) Stockhausen *Gesang der Junglinge (*Song of the Young Boy*)* (1957) Bernstein *West Side Story* (1957) Early synthesizers built	First regular BBC TV service begins (1936) World War II (1939–45) *Sputnik*, first satellite launched by Russians (1957)
Beatles first single *Love Me Do* (1962) Motown music Berio *Sequenza III* (1966)	First man in space – Gagarin (1961) President Kennedy shot (1963) Martin Luther King, Jr. killed (1968) Americans put first men on the moon (1969)
Reich *Drumming* (1970-71) Heavy metal/Glam rock/Disco IRCAM opens in Paris (1978) Punk/Rap CDs invented	First supersonic flight by Concorde across the Atlantic (1976) Wreck of *Titanic* found (1985) Berlin Wall comes down (1989)
Glass opera *Akhnaten* (1984) "Live Aid" concert	Nelson Mandela released from prison (1990)
House/Rave music	War in Yugoslavia (1992)

The scene at the end of Puccini's opera Madame Butterfly. *Madame Butterfly lies dead while Pinkerton comes to claim his child.*

AT THE END OF THE 19th century and the beginning of the 20th, many composers continued to write music in the Romantic style. Works by these late Romantics include the symphonies of Gustav Mahler, the operas of Giacomo Puccini and Richard Strauss, and the oratorios and symphonies of Edward Elgar. But at the same time, new styles and new ideas were being tried out by other composers. These new ideas opened up the possibilities of the modern age.

Debussy and the gamelan orchestra

The French composer Claude Debussy.

In 1889, Claude Debussy visited the Paris Exposition. This was the huge exhibition for which Gustave Eiffel built his famous tower. At this exhibition there was an Indonesian gamelan orchestra (see pages 36–37), and Debussy was fascinated by the sound of the gongs, the complex rhythms, and the strange scales that he heard. Debussy experimented in his own music with these new sounds and rhythms, producing music that was quite different from that of the Romantic composers. In his orchestral piece *La mer* ("The Sea"), written in 1905, Debussy used subtle rhythms and unusual scales.

Uproar at the ballet

In 1913, some people in the fashionable audience at a Paris theater were so upset by what they heard from the orchestra and saw on stage that some walked out and others started to shout and fight. The piece that caused this uproar was a ballet, *The Rite of Spring,* by Igor Stravinsky. The subject of the ballet shocked the audience–a ritual celebrating the coming of spring in which a young girl dances herself to death. The music also shocked them, most of all because Stravinsky used irregular rhythms, often changing the time signature (see page 86) almost every bar. This use of rhythm was an important influence on many 20th-century composers.

The Eiffel Tower was built for the 1889 Paris Exposition.

The age of jazz

A saxophonist in New Orleans, the birthplace of jazz music.

In the South of the United States, another new type of music was born at the beginning of the 20th century, called jazz. Jazz grew out of the many kinds of music that was played by people in the city of New Orleans, Louisiana. Two of the most important influences on early jazz were the blues and ragtime. The blues was a kind of folk music, sung by the descendants of the slaves brought from Africa to work on large plantations in the South. The words of blues songs were often about sadness and loneliness. Ragtime was a kind of piano music. Unlike the blues, it was often written down. Scott Joplin was a famous ragtime composer who wrote *The Entertainer* and *Elite Syncopations*.

Jazz music is often based on a tune called the theme. The performers play through the theme together to start, and then each player takes it in turns to make up a solo based on the theme. The piece often ends up with all the performers playing the theme together again.

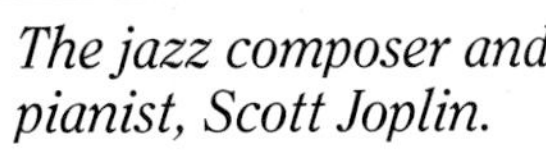

The jazz composer and pianist, Scott Joplin.

Messiaen's bird music

Olivier Messiaen collected birdsongs from all parts of his native France.

Olivier Messiaen was a French composer who is known especially for his organ music and his huge orchestral work, the *Turangalîla* Symphony, which features the strange electric instrument called the ondes martenot (see page 47). One of Messiaen's first loves was birdsongs. He traveled all around France to listen to birdsongs. He collected the songs not with a tape recorder but by writing them down, and he used birdsong music in many of his pieces.

Key facts

Music that experiments with ostinato effects is often known as minimalist music.

The American composer Steve Reich has studied techniques of African drumming.

Ostinato music

When a group of notes or a certain rhythm is repeated over and over again, it is called an ostinato (see page 85). Many musicians have experimented with ostinato effects, including the composers Steve Reich, John Adams, and Philip Glass. Reich, like many composers before him, is influenced by the subtle rhythms of the Indonesian gamelan orchestra as well as by African drumming. His piece *Drumming* uses ostinato effects on drums, glockenspiels, and marimba (a large xylophone). Philip Glass has studied Indian music, and he uses slowly changing ostinato patterns in his music, too. He has written an opera called *Akhnaten* about ancient Egypt.

Rock and pop music

One of the major developments in the music of the 20th century has been that of rock and pop music. Of course there has always been "popular" music, but the invention of recording and broadcasting has meant that people all over the world can now listen to the same music. There are many

A performance of Philip Glass's opera Akhnaten.

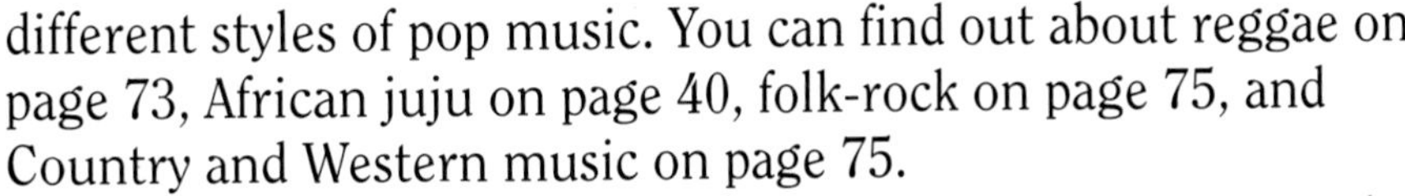

Diana Ross and the Supremes were Motown artists singing catchy and popular tunes.

different styles of pop music. You can find out about reggae on page 73, African juju on page 40, folk-rock on page 75, and Country and Western music on page 75.

Heavy metal dates from the late 1960s. Heavy metal bands play at an extremely loud volume, often using a piercing electronic sound called feedback caused by playing electric guitar in front of a loudspeaker. Heavy metal bands include AC/DC, Iron Maiden, and Black Sabbath.

Motown music originated in the city of Detroit, Michigan, which has a large car manufacturing industry (motortown). Record companies in Detroit promoted the Motown sound which was tuneful and catchy. Motown was very popular in the 1960s. Motown artists include Diana Ross and the Supremes and Stevie Wonder.

Rap became popular during the 1980s. Rap music uses a drum machine drumbeat, "scratching," which is done by dragging the needle of a record player across a record, and rhythmic talking over the top. Artists include the Beastie Boys and Grandmaster Flash.

Glam rock in 1973. David Bowie on stage.

Spectacular costumes and stage acts are often just as important in **glam rock** as the music. Famous glam rockers include David Bowie, Sweet, Spandau Ballet, and Bon Jovi.

Osibisa has had success not only in Africa, but around the world, because of the growing popularity of what is known as World music.

Disco music is dance music with a heavy beat. Disco music was popular in the 1970s, but other forms of dance music have since taken over, such as acid house and rave music. Disco greats include the Bee Gees, who provided the soundtrack for the film *Saturday Night Fever*.

Punk was partly a reaction to the sophisticated sounds of the disco music of the 1970s. It was meant to shock. Famous punk artists include The Sex Pistols.

Many musicians in the West have become interested in the music of other cultures. Some musicians have mixed in elements from these cultures with their own music. And some African and Arab musicians have had successful record releases in the West, including Youssou N'Dour, Ofra Haza, and Osibisa. This kind of music is known as **World music**.

Every year carolers sing traditional Christmas carols.

Folk music

SOME TUNES THAT ARE WELL-KNOWN today are very old. Many Christmas carols, for example, are based on tunes and words that have been sung for hundreds of years. Often no one knows who wrote these tunes or where they came from. They have been sung and played by generation after generation, changing slightly as they have been passed down through history. This is folk music.

Working songs

People from different countries and cultures have their own traditions of folk music. But although a folk song from Japan and one from South America might sound very different, the subjects that people sing about are often similar. In folk-music traditions all over the world, there are working songs, songs about love, everyday life, the seasons, battles and war, shepherd's songs, cradle songs, and many more.

Key facts

Music of the church and the court is often known as "art" music. Music sung by the ordinary people that is not usually written down but passed on and changed from one generation to the next is often known as "folk" music.

Shanties

Some of the most well-known working songs were sung at sea by sailors working on sailing ships. These songs are called shanties. Shanties were sung by sailors as they hauled on the ropes that hoisted the sails. The rhythm of the songs helped the sailors to pull together and to raise the sail more easily. There were also shanties for other jobs on board ship, such as

All over the world fishermen have their own songs to help them pull in their nets.

Gospel music developed in the United States from the spirituals sung by slaves.

pulling up the anchor. In North America the fur traders who lived in the far north sang songs as they paddled their canoes across the icy seas. Often the song would last as long as the journey lasted, sometimes from morning to night!

Working the land

On land many working songs helped people to forget their aches and pains as they toiled in the fields. Often these songs were about the crops being tended or the animals being looked after. Shepherds sang about their sheep and lambs and about the bitter weather they must endure out in the fields. In Japan there are many songs about rice-growing because rice was one of the main ingredients of the Japanese diet. Rice-planting songs have words about putting in the rice seedlings and how much rice they will produce. Many of these folk songs are still sung today in Japan, especially at festivals and celebrations.

Spirituals

Spirituals were religious songs sung by the black slaves working on the plantations in the southern United States in the 19th century. Spirituals were sung in church or in the fields as the slaves worked. A leader would sing one line to which the rest of the singers responded, another line and another response, and so on. The words of the spiritual songs often reflected the hard life of the slaves. Spirituals such as Sometimes I Feel Like a Motherless Child and Nobody Knows the Trouble I've Seen were sometimes called "sorrow songs." The same "call and response" is used today by evangelical worshipers and is known as gospel music.

A rice-planting festival in Osaka, Japan. Traditional rice-planting songs are still sung in some parts of Japan.

Chinese opera

Like opera in the West (see page 55), Chinese opera is a mixture of music and drama. The opera performed at the emperor's court was very formal, sometimes lasting five or six hours. A rather different form of opera was popular with the ordinary Chinese people. Chinese folk opera often included acrobatics and mime, as well as dancing and singing. Performers were trained to sing and dance and to perform acrobatics.

A character from a Chinese folk opera.

Music for entertainment

Once the day's work was over, it was time for some entertainment. In Scotland before the 18th century, rich families in the Highlands paid for a storyteller, called a bard, to live as one of the household. The job of the bard was to sing and tell stories in the evenings for the entertainment of the family and their guests. Sometimes the bards were accompanied by the clarsach, a small harp, played by skilled harpists who traveled from place to place visiting the wealthy Scottish families. For dancing, a fiddler would play to accompany the whirling dances known as reels. Reels are still danced today.

Whirling Scottish dances are known as reels.

The late Bob Marley is the most famous of all reggae musicians.

Reggae

Reggae comes from the island of Jamaica in the Caribbean. The rhythms and instruments of reggae show influences not only from Jamaican music, but from Africa and America, too. The most famous of all reggae musicians was Bob Marley, who made this style of music internationally known in the 1970s.

Dancing

Folk tunes were often used as music for dancing. People danced for entertainment, for celebrations, during religious ceremonies, and on many other occasions, and they still do! You may have seen local folk dances such as Morris dancing or maypole dances.

Every country has its own traditions of folk music and dancing, and when people from one country move to a new part of the world, they take their traditions with them. The music and dances of the Caribbean region show the influence of the local peoples and all the various people who settled there. In the 16th century people from many European countries colonized the islands, and from the 16th to the 19th centuries, African slaves were brought to work on plantations in the region. The music and the instruments of the Caribbean reflect all these different influences. For example, on one of the Caribbean islands, the Dominican Republic, Congo groups play music that mixes African drumming styles with Spanish-type melodies.

Collecting folk music

In many places traditional folk songs and dances have been dying out since machines began to take over the work once done by hand. But at the beginning of the 20th century, some composers and musicians became interested in folk traditions and tried to record folk tunes before they died out. The composers Béla Bartók and Zoltán Kodály traveled around Hungary recording folk music. Bartók took with him a simple recorder into which people sang or played. Bartók would then

Béla Bartók traveled around Hungary with his fellow composer, Zoltán Kodály, collecting folk music.

listen to the recording and write down the notes that he heard. Between them, Kodály and Bartók collected about 15,000 tunes, and the influence of Hungarian folk music can be heard in their own music. Another composer, Leoš Janáček, collected the folk music of his native Czechoslovakia, and in Britain Ralph Vaughan Williams, Gustav Holst, and Cecil Sharp all made folk music collections.

The development of folk festivals and music

There are many festivals of folk music, but one of the most famous is the eisteddfod held every year in Llangollen, Wales. In medieval times gatherings of bards met to discuss music and literature. The eisteddfod developed from these meetings. At the International Eisteddfod, folk choirs and dancers from all over the world compete for prizes.

There is also a National Eisteddfod held annually in different places in Wales, which gives prestigious prizes for choral singing and other music.

Although many traditional folk tunes have been forgotten, folk music is still sung and played all over the world. One of the main features of folk music is that it is changing all the time. Even when folk music is written down, folk musicians invent new words, add decorations to the tune, or perform the music slightly differently each time. In many parts of the world, the rhythms and tunes of traditional music have been adapted for more up-to-date instruments.

Bards at the Welsh National Eisteddfod in Aberystwyth, Wales.

A Country and Western singer plays the guitar to accompany himself when singing.

Country and Western music

Country and Western music has its roots in the folk music of North America, although it is popular all over the world. Early styles of Country and Western music used the tunes of folk songs and dances accompanied by banjos, guitars, violins, and mouth organs. In the 1950s a new instrument–the Hawaiian guitar–was added. This was a type of electric guitar that made an unusual sliding sound when the player dragged a piece of metal along the strings. Today Country and Western bands still use the Hawaiian guitar as well as other electric instruments. You will probably know the names of some Country and Western stars, such as Garth Brooks, Dolly Parton, and Bonnie Raitt.

Folk groups

Many singers and groups still perform traditional folk music, often now with the accompaniment of electric instruments. In the 1960s a type of music called folk-rock became popular. Folk-rock music combined the melodies of folk music with the sound of the electric bass guitar and the drum kit. Often the words of folk-rock songs carried a political message. Bob Dylan is probably the most famous folk-rock musician. Here are some other folk and folk-rock singers and groups for you to listen to: Simon and Garfunkel, Fairport Convention, Steeleye Span, Ralph McTell, Richard Thompson, June Tabor, The Chieftains, Pete Seeger, and The Weavers.

Many of Bob Dylan's songs have a political message.

Pulse and rhythm

Finding the pulse

A pulse is a steady beat. You can find your own pulse on the inside of your wrist or on your neck underneath your jawbone. This regular beat is caused by your heart pumping blood around your body. Many everyday things also have a pulse, for example, the regular ticking of a clock or the beeping of an alarm clock.

The steady beats of music are grouped together, most commonly into twos, threes, and fours. When music is written down, the groups are divided into bars, separated by barlines, with the first beat in each bar usually being the strongest.

1 2 3 4 | 1 2 3 4

1 2 3 | 1 2 3 | 1 2 3

1 2 | 1 2 | 1 2 | 1 2

Clapping the beat

You could try inventing a "pulse piece" with a couple of friends. It works like this: person one claps the steady pulse grouped in threes or fours. For example, use a pulse grouped in fours. Person two claps on beats 1 and 4. Person three claps on beats 1 and 3. Try the same method with different pulse groups. This gives you an idea of how music starts to be formed.

Person 1. ♩ ♩ ♩ ♩ | ♩ ♩ ♩ ♩ | ♩ ♩ ♩ ♩

Person 2. ♩ ♩ | ♩ ♩ | ♩ ♩

Person 3. ♩ ♩ | ♩ ♩ | ♩ ♩

Working out the beat

Listen to different pieces of music to see if you can work out how the beats are grouped. Here are some examples of songs you may know and what pulse they have:

$\frac{2}{2}$ What shall we do with the drunken sailor

$\frac{3}{4}$ Close every / door to me (from *Joseph and His Amazing Technicolor Dreamcoat* by Andrew Lloyd Webber)

$\frac{4}{4}$ We all live in a / yellow submarine (by the Beatles)

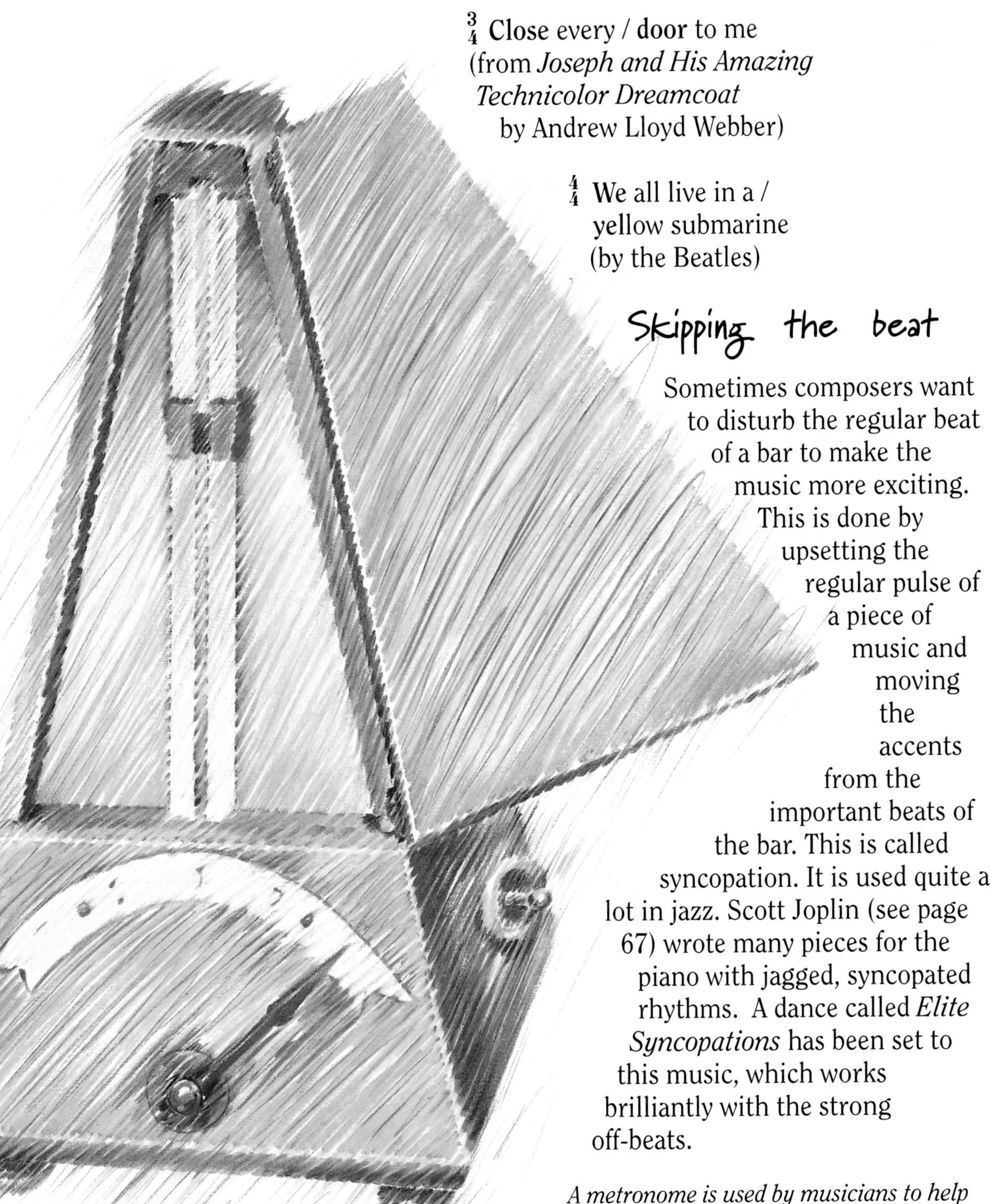

Skipping the beat

Sometimes composers want to disturb the regular beat of a bar to make the music more exciting. This is done by upsetting the regular pulse of a piece of music and moving the accents from the important beats of the bar. This is called syncopation. It is used quite a lot in jazz. Scott Joplin (see page 67) wrote many pieces for the piano with jagged, syncopated rhythms. A dance called *Elite Syncopations* has been set to this music, which works brilliantly with the strong off-beats.

A metronome is used by musicians to help them keep to a steady pulse. It can be set to different speeds.

There are many kinds of dances to lots of different rhythms. This dance is a tango, and the rhythm is syncopated.

Rhythm

As you sing, play, or listen to music, you will notice that there is more to it than just a steady beat. There are notes that are shorter and longer than one beat. When all the notes of varying length are put together, the music has a rhythm. Sometimes the rhythm of the music has a strong, steady beat or pulse. At other times there will only be a weak pulse, or there may even be no pulse at all.

The rhythm of a piece is written down in notes. These are some of the most common notes:

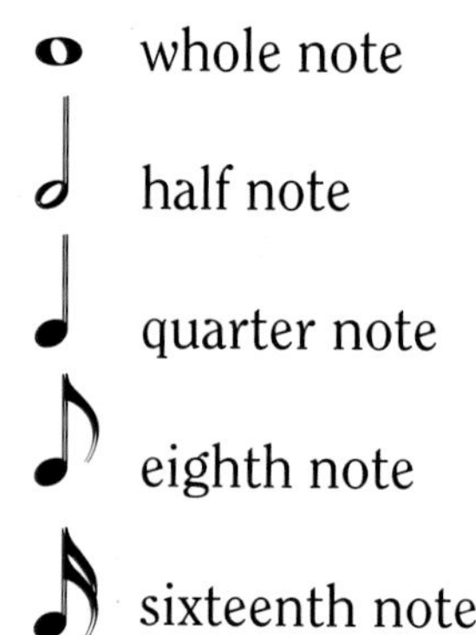

whole note

half note

quarter note

eighth note

sixteenth note

The names for the notes are on the right. These names show how long the notes are compared to each other. The whole note lasts twice as long as the half note; a half note lasts twice as long as a quarter note and so on.

Key facts

Eighth notes and sixteenth notes are joined together into groups if there is more than one of them. For example, two eighth notes are equal to one quarter note:

♫ = ♩

and four sixteenth notes are equal to one quarter note:

♬♬ = ♩

You can mix up different kinds of notes in one beat group. For example, one eighth note and two sixteenth notes are equal to one quarter note:

♪♬ = ♩

The time signature

At the beginning of a piece of music, there are two numbers, one above the other. This is called the time signature, and it explains two things. The top number tells you how many beats there are in each bar of the piece. The bottom number tells you which note is considered to be the beat. If a time signature says $\frac{2}{4}$, there are two beats in each bar, and the beats are quarter notes (the 4 referring to a quarter note). If the time signature says $\frac{3}{2}$, there are three beats in each bar, and the beats are half notes (the 2 referring to a half note). Examples of rhythms in these times can be seen in the box on page 79.

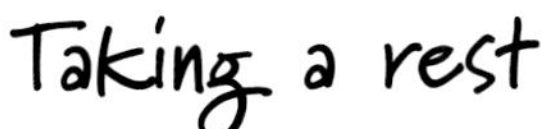

Taking a rest

In music the silences are just as important as the notes, especially if you are singing or playing a wind or brass instrument–you need to take a breath every now and then! The silences, or rests, can have different lengths just like notes. They are written down like this:

a whole-note 𝅝 rest looks like this: 𝄻

a half-note 𝅗𝅥 rest looks like this: 𝄼

a quarter-note ♩ rest looks like this: 𝄽

a eighth-note ♪ rest looks like this: 𝄾

a sixteenth-note 𝅘𝅥𝅯 rest looks like this: 𝄿

Going dotty

𝅝. = 1½ whole notes
𝅗𝅥. = 1½ half notes
♩. = 1½ quarter notes
♪. = 1½ eighth notes
𝅘𝅥𝅯. = 1½ sixteenth notes

Sometimes you might want a note to last longer than one beat but less than two beats. To make a note last 1½ beats, it should be written down with a dot next to it like this: ♩. The note is a quarter note, and the dot adds on half the value of the note it is beside. You can put a dot next to any kind of note, and it will always make the note worth half as much again.

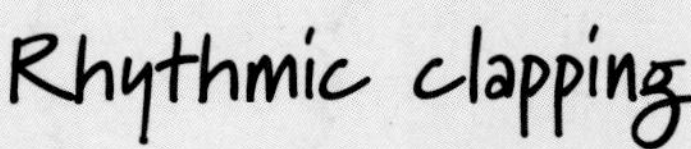

Rhythmic clapping

With a friend, try clapping these rhythms. The first person claps:

2/4 ♩ ♩ | ♩ ♩ | ♩ ♩ | ♩ ♩

The second person claps:

2/4 ♩ ♩ | 𝅗𝅥 | ♫ ♫ | 𝅗𝅥

In bar 2, the half note lasts for the same amount of time as two quarter notes. So the first person will clap twice, while the second person will clap once and wait.

Now try these rhythms.

3/2 𝅗𝅥 𝅗𝅥 𝅗𝅥 | 𝅗𝅥 𝅗𝅥 𝅗𝅥 | 𝅗𝅥 𝅗𝅥 𝅗𝅥 | 𝅗𝅥 𝅗𝅥 𝅗𝅥

3/2 𝅗𝅥 𝅗𝅥 ♩ ♩ | 𝅗𝅥 𝅗𝅥 ♩ ♫ | 𝅗𝅥 𝅗𝅥 𝅗𝅥 | 𝅗𝅥 𝅝

In bar 4, the whole note lasts for the same amount of time as two half notes. So the first person will clap twice and the second person once and wait.

Make up your own rhythms and perhaps try them out on percussion instruments.

What makes music work is not just the rhythm but also the tune. Here choristers sing music that is written in many parts.

Pitch and melody

PULSE AND RHYTHM ARE NOT the only things that make up a piece of music. Most popular pieces also have a good tune.

Melodies tend to go up and down in a mixture of steps and leaps, and it is the balance of steps and leaps that makes for a memorable tune. Imagine a staircase of steps, numbered one, two, three, four, and so on, from the bottom upward. You could describe a melody by the number of the step, but although the numbers would tell you how the notes are arranged into a melody, they would not tell you about the rhythm of the music. If you want to be absolutely clear about the pitches and the rhythm of your tune, then you have to use a more precise system of writing music down. Today music is usually written down using five lines, called a staff.

A staff is used to write musical notes on. Each line and each space between the lines represents different pitches.

Shapes in melodies

When the notes of a tune are written on the staff, they show you not only the pitch and the rhythm of the melody but also its shape. Some bits of a melody may be repeated; other bits may be different to provide contrast.

Many songs fall into a pattern of repeating one idea (A), slotting in a new idea for contrast (B), and then repeating the first idea again (A). This gives many melodies the shape AABA. It makes inventing melodies much easier when you realize that you really need only two musical ideas!

The treble clef

At the beginning of every piece of written music, there is a clef. This acts as a reference point for music, because without a clef you cannot say what the pitch of any written note is. The treble clef, or G clef, shows that the second line up in the staff is a G. The center of the clef curls around the second line up. In the middle of the piano keyboard is the note Middle C. The treble clef also tells you that any note you put onto the second line up will sound as the pitch of the first G you come to above Middle C.

In music the first seven letters of the alphabet are used to describe notes. As you move up the staff, you go higher in pitch and forward through the alphabet using all the lines and spaces on the staff. When all seven letters are used up, start again at A. If you want to write Middle C on the staff, you have to add an extra line. This is called a ledger line.

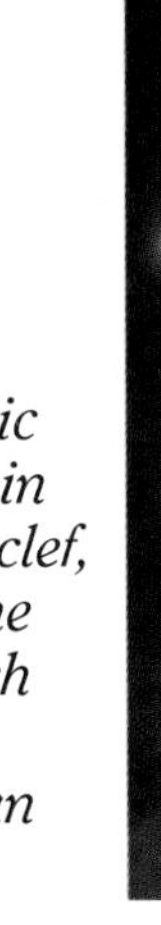

A flautist reads music that is set in the treble clef, because the flute's pitch range is higher than Middle C.

The bass clef

To show that the pitch of the notes on the staff are below Middle C, the bass clef, or F clef, is used. The bass clef shows that the second line down on the staff is an F, the F below Middle C. The two dots sit on either side of the F line.

If you look at some music written for the piano, you will usually see two staffs, joined together, the top staff with a treble clef and the bottom staff with a bass clef. The staff with the treble clef is usually played with the right hand, and the staff with the bass clef is usually played with the left hand.

Other instruments use the clef that is most suited to their pitch range. A flautist reads music in a treble clef because the notes the flute can play are all above Middle C. A double bass player reads music in the bass clef because most of the notes the double bass can play are lower than Middle C.

A double bass player reads music written in the bass clef because the double bass produces notes below Middle C.

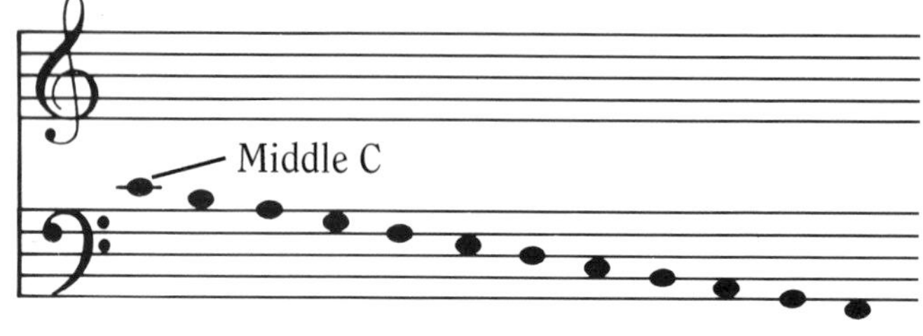

Tones and semitones

On the piano keyboard, when you move stepwise from one note to the very next note, this distance is called a semitone (or half step). The distance between B and C is a semitone; the distance between D and the black note immediately above it is also a semitone. The distance of two semitones is called a tone (or whole step), for example F to G, or C to D.

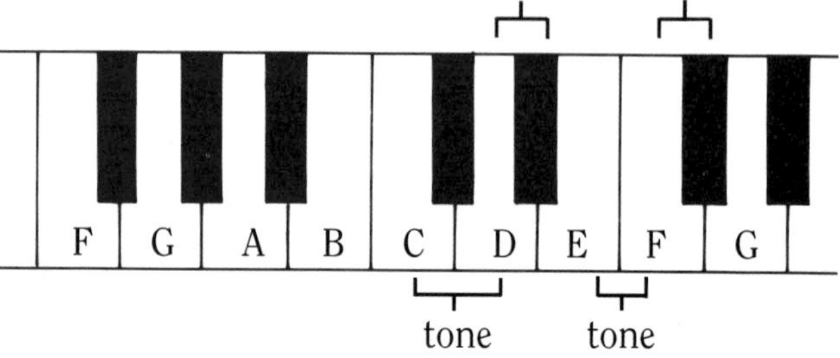

A pianist playing the piano. The right hand usually plays above Middle C in the treble clef, and the left hand usually plays below Middle C in the bass clef.

When you see a sharp sign (#) in front of a note, it means that you raise the note by a semitone. So if you see F#, you would play this black note on the piano keyboard:

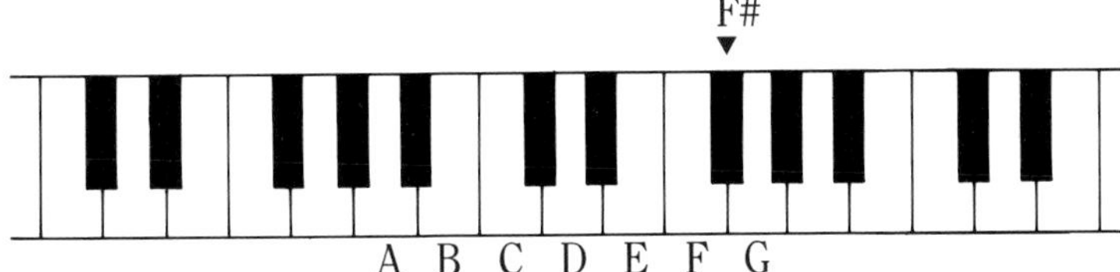

When you see a flat sign (♭) in front of a note, it means that you lower the note by a semitone. So if you see B♭, you would play this black note on the piano keyboard:

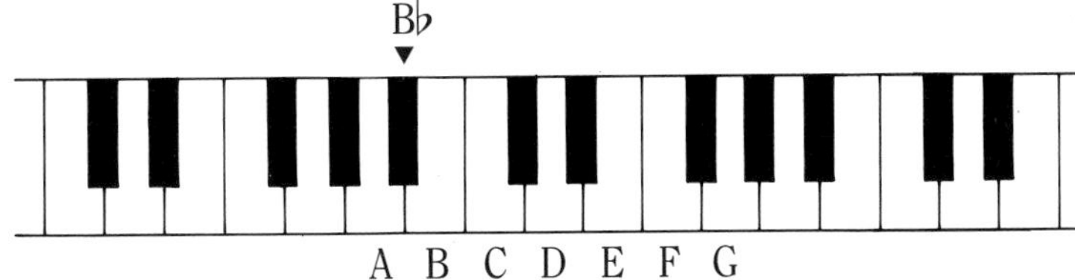

Scales

A scale is a series of notes arranged in order of rising or descending pitches. There are many different kinds of scales. For example, a pentatonic scale is made up of five notes, such as C, D, E, G, A or G, A, C, D, E. A raga is another kind of scale used in Indian music. Most Western music is based on major or minor scales. A major scale is a succession of notes rising stepwise with the following pattern of intervals: tone, tone, semitone, tone, tone, tone, semitone.

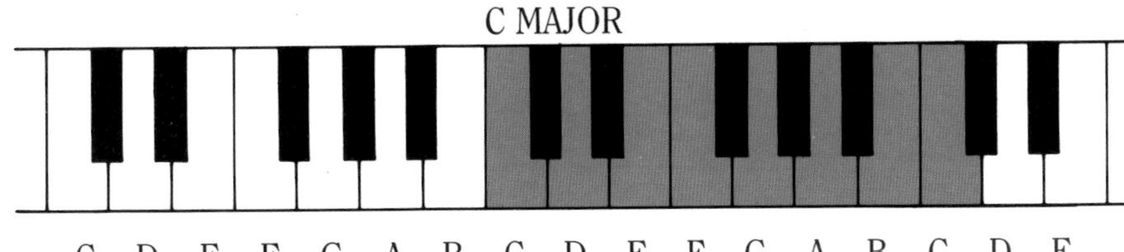

A minor scale is a succession of notes rising stepwise with this pattern of intervals: tone, semitone, tone, tone, semitone, tone, tone. It does not matter what note you start on so long as you follow the pattern.

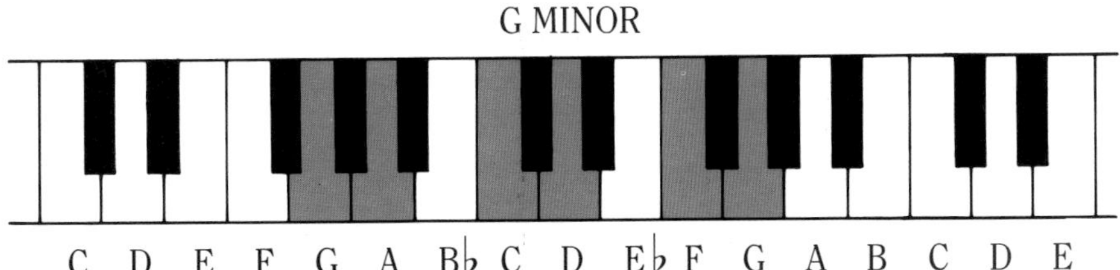

A piece of music that is based on the scale of C major is said to be in the key of C major. A piece of music that is based on the scale of G minor is said to be in the key of G minor.

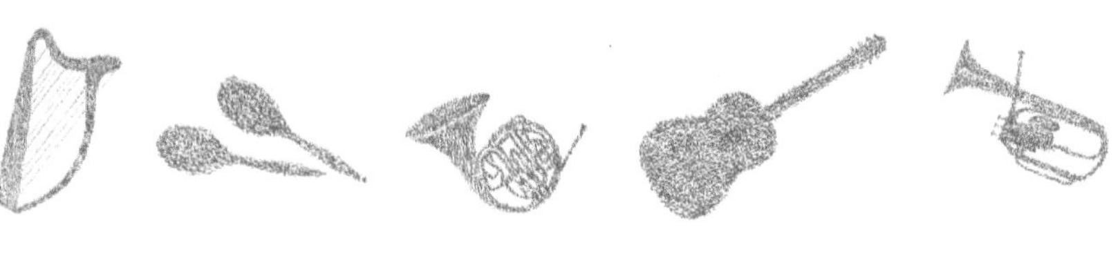

Glossary of musical terms

accent > a note that is emphasized.
bar a group of beats defined by barlines.
barline the vertical lines on the staff, used to divide groups of beats.
binary form a piece of music is said to be in binary form when it consists of two sections (A and B). Often each section is repeated (AABB).
chord two or more notes played together.
clef the treble clef or (G clef) 𝄞 shows you that the second line up on the staff is the G above Middle C. The bass clef (F clef) 𝄢 shows you that the second line down on the staff is the F below Middle C.
coda an extra section of music that is sometimes added to the end of a piece to reinforce the conclusion.
concerto a composition for orchestra and a solo instrument, or group of solo instruments.
double barline the pair of vertical lines that appear at the end of the last bar of a piece of music.
drone a long sustained note (or notes), or a repeated note.
dynamic markings the words and signs that indicate the way a piece should be played or sung. (For example–pp, f, crescendo: see box on page 87.)
flat the sign ♭. When this sign appears before a note, it tells you that the note is lowered by a semitone. For example:

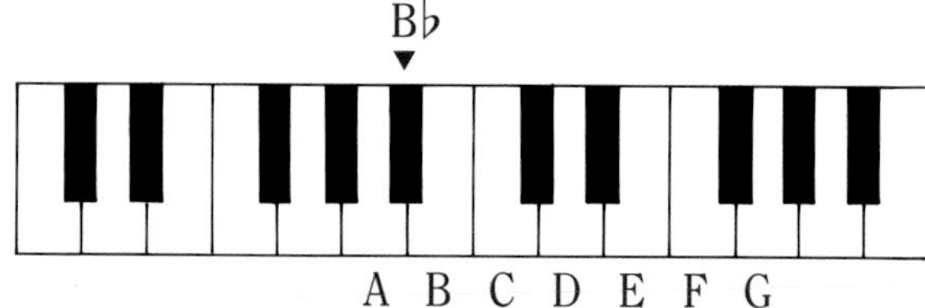

form the structure of a piece of music; how the musical ideas are organized.
fret a thin piece of metal that crosses the fingerboard of some string instruments to show you where to place your fingers on the strings (for example, on a guitar, a lute, and a banjo).
improvise to make up music as you play it.
interval the distance from one note to another.

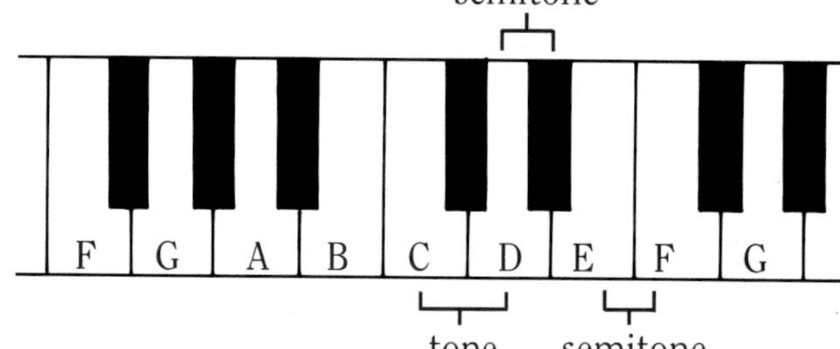

The interval between one note and the very next note is called a semitone, or half step. For example:

E to F is a semitone
A to B♭ is a semitone
C to C# is a semitone
B to C is a semitone.

The interval made up of two semitones is called a tone, or whole step. For example:

A to B is a tone
D♭ to E♭ is a tone
E to F# is a tone
F to G is a tone.

The distance between the notes C and E is called an interval of a 3rd.
The distance between the notes C and G is called an interval of a 5th.
The distance between the notes C and A is called an interval of a 6th.
The distance between the notes C and the next C above is called an octave (meaning an 8th).
key the scale on which a piece of music is based. For example, a piece of music using the notes C, D, E, F, G, A, B, C could be said to be in the key of C major.
key signature the sharps (#) or flats (♭) that appear at the beginning of each staff to tell you which key the piece is in, and therefore which notes to make sharp or flat.

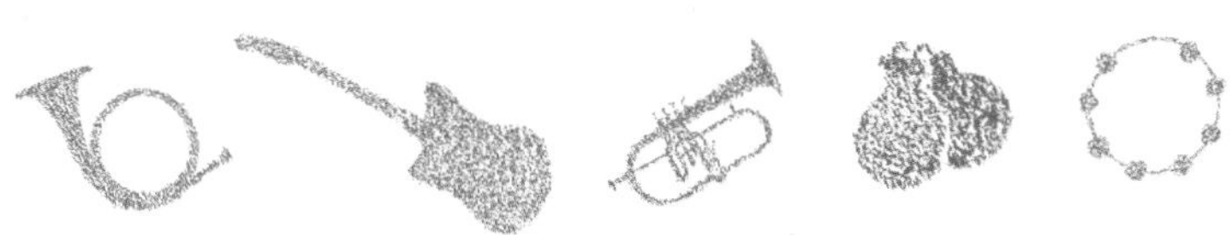

ledger lines extra, short lines for notes above or below the staff.

major a piece that is based on a major scale is said to be in a major key.

major scale a succession of notes moving stepwise in the following pattern of intervals: tone, tone, semitone, tone, tone, tone, semitone. For example, the scale of C major contains the notes C, D, E, F, G, A, B, C.

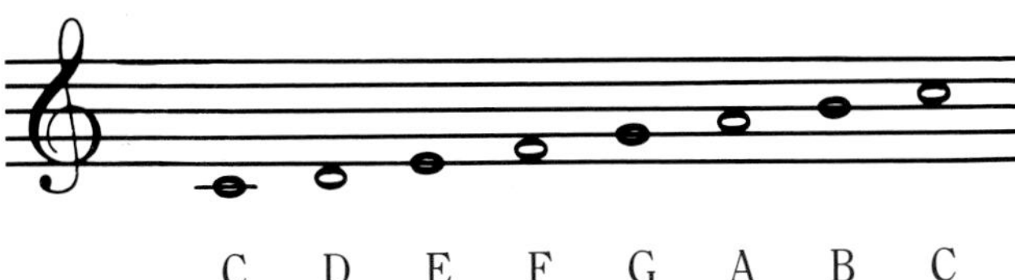

C D E F G A B C

The interval between C and D is a tone.
The interval between D and E is a tone.
The interval between E and F is a semitone.
The interval between F and G is a tone.
The interval between G and A is a tone.
The interval between A and B is a tone.
The interval between B and C is a semitone.

The notes of a major scale starting on the note D would be: D, E, F#, G, A, B, C#, D. This is the scale of D major.

D E F# G A B C# D

In this scale you have to introduce some sharps (#) in order to follow the pattern of intervals.

minor a piece that is based on a minor scale is said to be in a minor key.

minor scale a succession of notes moving stepwise in the following pattern of intervals: tone, semitone, tone, tone, semitone, tone, tone. For example, the scale of A minor contains the notes A, B, C, D, E, F, G, A.

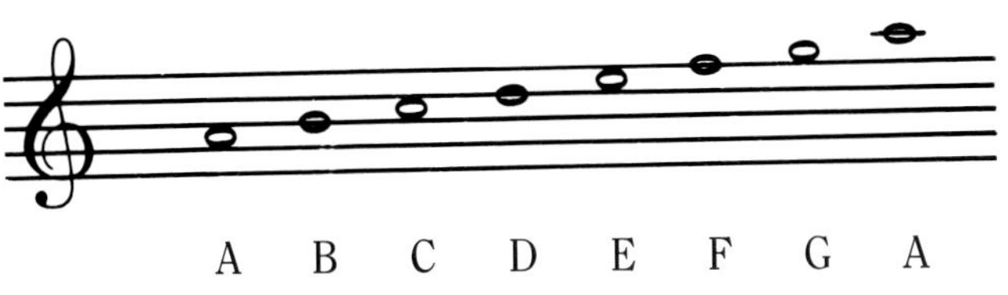

A B C D E F G A

The interval between A and B is a tone.
The interval between B and C is a semitone.
The interval between C and D is a tone.
The inetrval between D and E is a tone.
The interval between E and F is a semitone.
The interval between F and G is a tone.
The interval between G and A is a tone.

The notes of a minor scale starting on the note G would be: G, A, B♭, C, D, E♭, F, G
This is the scale of G minor.

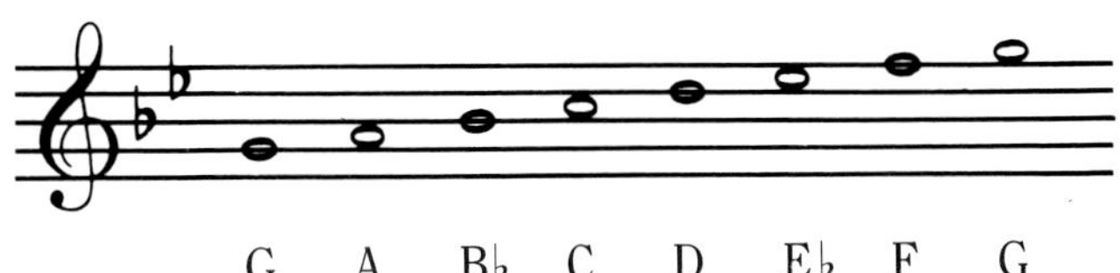

G A B♭ C D E♭ F G

In this scale you have to introduce some flats (♭) in order to follow the pattern of intervals.

mode there are several different modes, each based on a different pattern of intervals.

modulation a change of key during a piece of music.

natural shown by the sign ♮. When this sign appears before a note, it shows that you do not sharpen or flatten the note. For example, if you want to write an F and the key signature contains an F#, you need to put a natural sign (♮) in front of the F to stop it from being altered.

notation the methods used to write music down.

octave the interval of an 8th–for example, from Middle C to the C above it.

ostinato a repeating melodic and/or rhythmic idea that continues persistently throughout a piece (or part of a piece) of music.

pause the sign 𝄐 over a note or a rest that tells you that the note or rest should be prolonged.

pentatonic music that is based on a five-note scale, such as C, D, E, G, A; or C, D, F, G, A; or G, A, C, D, E.

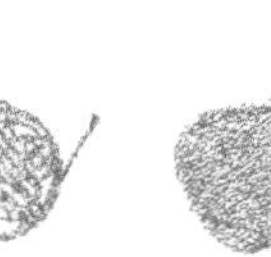

phrase a phrase in music is rather like a phrase in language. Just as two or more phrases separated by commas help to make up a sentence, so several musical phrases make up a piece of music. Musical phrases are often indicated by phrase marks:

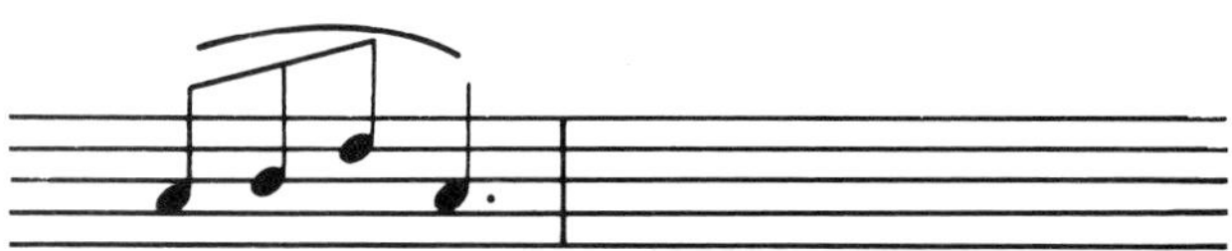

pitch how high or how low a note is. (The exact pitch of a note is determined by the number of vibrations per second.)
pulse a regular beat.
raga a scale on which a piece of Indian music is improvised.
rest a symbol meaning silence. Each note value has an equivalent rest symbol (see page 79).
rondo a musical form in which the ideas are organized in the pattern A-B-A-C-A-D-A so the musical idea A keeps repeating, with other episodes between.
round a song that is sung in several parts. Each part begins at the beginning, but the parts do not begin together (for example "London's Burning" and "Frère Jacques").
scale a pattern of intervals arranged in order of rising pitches (see major, minor, pentatonic, whole tone).
Scotch snap a dotted rhythm that is found in much traditional Scottish music, for example, a strathspey. The short note is always first:

semitone the distance between one note and the very next note (see page 82).
sharp shown by the sign # before a note. It tells you that the note is raised by a semitone.

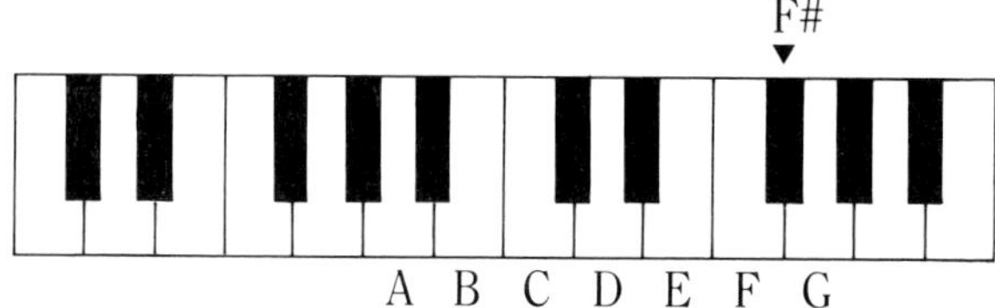

staff the five lines on which you write musical notes.
symphony a composition for orchestra with three or four separate sections called movements.
syncopation when the regular pulse of a piece of music is interrupted by moving the accents from the important beats of the bar. For example:

ternary form a piece of music in ternary form would follow the pattern ABA. In other words, the same musical idea would appear at the beginning and the end of the piece, with something different in the middle–like a sandwich that has bread on either side of a filling in the middle!
tie a curved line that is used to join two notes of the same pitch that are separated by a barline. For example:

You would hold the third note for three beats.
time signature the two numbers that appear one above the other at the beginning of a piece of music. The top number tells how many beats there are in a bar. The bottom number tells what kind of note the beat is (see page 78).
tone the distance of two semitones (see page 82).

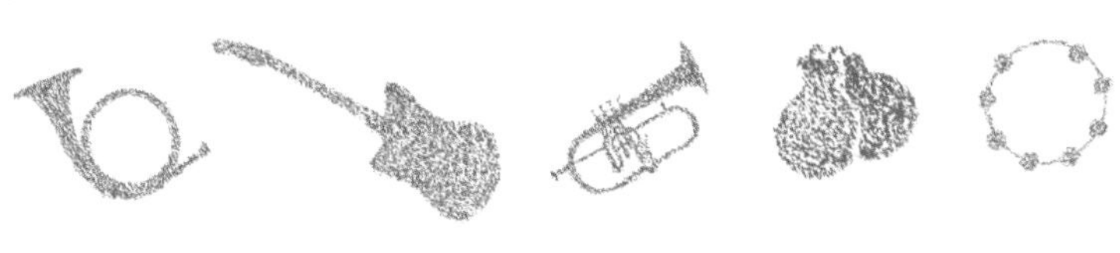

upbeat one or more notes that begin before the first barline. For example:

valves modern trumpets have three valves. If the player presses one of the valves down, the air in the trumpet travels through an extra length of tubing. This makes the column of air longer and produces a lower note. Tubas and French horns also have valves.

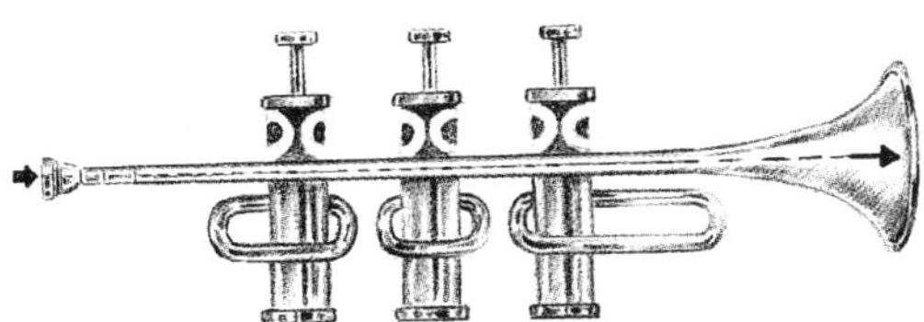

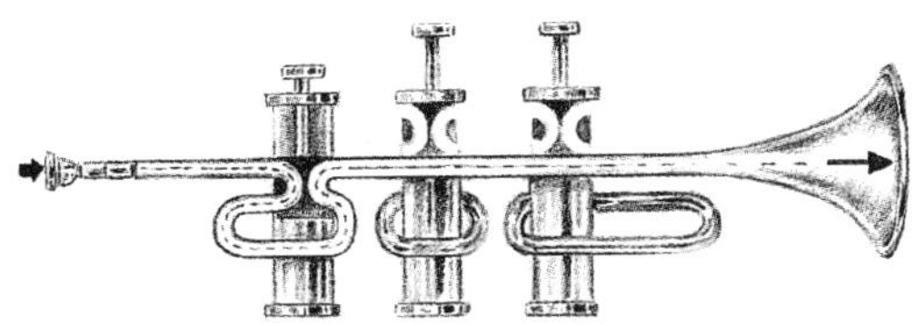

whole-tone scale a series of notes that form a scale. Each note is a tone higher than the previous one. For example:

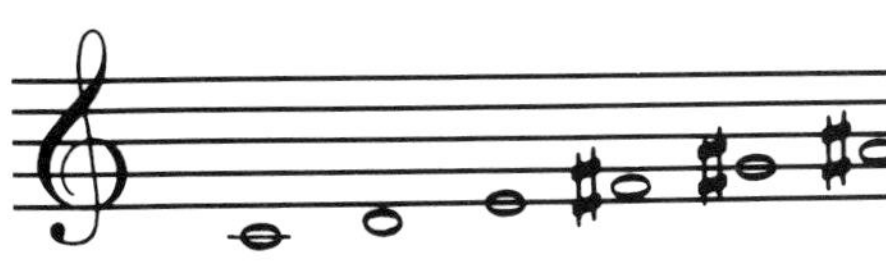

This gives a very open-ended sound, and music based on a whole-tone scale sounds very different from any other.

Italian terms

Most composers use Italian terms to tell the performer how they would like their music to be sung or played. Here are some of the most common terms:

accelerando (or **accel.**) gradually getting faster.
adagio slow.
allegretto quite quick (but not as quick as allegro).
allegro quick.
andante at a walking pace.
arco this is a direction to string players to use the bow instead of plucking the strings.
cantabile in a singing style.
crescendo (or **cresc.** <) gradually getting louder.
da capo (or **D.C.**) repeat from the beginning.
dal segno (or **D.S.**) go back to the sign 𝄋 and repeat from there.
decrescendo (or **decresc.** <) gradually getting quieter.
diminuendo (or **dim.** <) gradually getting quieter.
fine the end.
f (stands for **forte**) loud.
ff (stands for **fortissimo**) very loud.
largo very slow.
legato (or **leg.**) smoothly.
lento slow.
mezzo half.
mf (stands for **mezzo forte**) moderately loud.
mp (stands for **mezzo piano**) moderately soft.
moderato at a moderate speed.
p (stands for **piano**) quiet.
pp (stands for **pianissimo**) very quiet.
pizzicato this is a direction to string players to pluck the strings with their fingers.
poco a little.
presto very fast.
rallentando (or **rall.**) getting gradually slower.
ritardando (or **ritard.**, or **rit.**) getting gradually slower.
ritenuto held back.
staccato (or **stacc.**) detached.
tempo speed.
vivace lively, quick.

A sheet from one of Bach's original manuscripts, written in 1708.

Glossary of composers

Adams, John (b. 1947) American composer and conductor. His works include the opera *Nixon in China.*

Bach, Johann Sebastian (1685–1750) German. One of the greatest composers, who came from a family of musicians. For much of his life, Bach worked at St. Thomas's Church and school in Leipzig where he composed music for church services, as well as works such as *St. John Passion, St. Matthew Passion,* and the setting in B minor of the Mass.

Barber, Samuel (1910–1981) American. One of America's most popular composers who wrote extensively for the voice, as well as for instrumental groups. His most famous work is probably the Adagio for strings (also arranged for voices).

Bartók, Béla (1881–1945) Hungarian composer and pianist. With Kodály, studied Hungarian folk music. His most famous works include the Concerto for Orchestra and the opera *Bluebeard's Castle*.

Beach, Amy Marcy (1867–1944) American. Pianist and composer who was the first president of the Association of Women Composers.

Beethoven, Ludwig van (1770–1827) German. Musical genius who spanned the end of the Classical and beginning of the Romantic periods. He wrote much chamber music including string quartets and piano music. He also composed nine symphonies, pushing the symphonic form to its limits. During the last 25 years of his life, he grew progressively more deaf.

Berio, Luciano (b. 1925) Italian composer. He has worked extensively with synthesizers and often mixes musical instruments with prerecorded tapes in his music.

Berlioz, Hector (1803–1869) French. Dramatic, Romantic composer who wrote many large-scale works including the huge setting of the Requiem Mass and the *Symphonie Fantastique* (Fantastic Symphony).

Bernstein, Leonard (1918–1990) American composer and conductor. Composer of *West Side Story*.

Bizet, Georges (1838–1875) French composer most famous for his opera *Carmen*.

Boulanger, Nadia (1887–1979) French. Teacher and composer. Her sister Lili Boulanger (1893–1918) was the first woman to win the music prize called the Grand Prix de Rome, awarded by the Academy of Fine Arts in Paris, France.

Boulez, Pierre (b. 1925) Composer and conductor. Involved in setting up computer music studio in Paris called IRCAM.

Brahms, Johannes (1833–1897) German. Romantic composer who wrote four symphonies as well as much chamber music.

Johannes Brahms

Britten, Benjamin (1913–1976) British composer and pianist. Famous for his operas such as *Peter Grimes, Albert Herring,* and *The Little Sweep*.

Bruckner, Anton (1824–1896) Austrian. Wrote nine symphonies as well as church music. Also an organist.

Byrd, William (c. 1542–1623) English composer who wrote music for both Catholic and Protestant services.

Cage, John (1912–1992) American. Experimental composer who has influenced many 20th-century musicians.

Chaminade, Cécile (1857–1944) French pianist and composer. She wrote many, mostly lighthearted, "salon" pieces for the piano as well as some larger-scale works.
Chopin, Frédéric (1810–1849) Polish. Piano virtuoso and composer, famous for his piano music.
Copland, Aaron (1900–1990) American. Influenced by Stravinsky but wrote music with an "American" feel, such as *Appalachian Spring*.
Davies, Peter Maxwell (b. 1934) British composer. Helped to set up St. Magnus Festival on islands of Orkney, Scotland, and has written many pieces to be performed there.
Debussy, Claude (1862–1918) French composer who has influenced many composers and musicians in the 20th century.
Delius, Frederick (1862–1934) British composer. Studied in Leipzig and lived for much of his life in Grez-sur-Loing, France. Well-known for his orchestral evocations of nature in such works as *On Hearing the First Cuckoo in Spring*.
Des Prez, Josquin (c. 1440–1521) Flemish. Born in northern France but worked in Italy for much of his life. He wrote 20 settings of the Catholic Mass.
Dufay, Guillaume (c. 1400–1474) Born in France. Composer who worked in the courts of France and Italy, traveling widely.
Dvořák, Antonin (1841–1904) Czech. Spent three years in America where he wrote the Ninth Symphony *From the New World*.
Elgar, Edward (1857–1934) British. Wrote many orchestral and choral works including *The Dream of Gerontius* and the *Enigma* variations.
Fauré, Gabriel (1845–1924) French. Wrote many songs and much piano music.
Gershwin, George (1898–1937) American. Composer who combined elements of jazz and classical music in works such as the opera Porgy and Bess and the orchestral piece Rhapsody in Blue.

George Gershwin

Glass, Philip (b. 1937) American. Studied among others with Nadia Boulanger and Ravi Shankar. Minimalist composer.
Grieg, Edvard (1843–1907) Norwegian composer. In much of his music, influenced by folk styles and tunes of Norwegian music. Most famous for the Piano Concerto in A minor, and the music for *Peer Gynt*.
Handel, George Frideric (1685–1759) German. Wrote many oratorios, including *Messiah*, as well as operas. Worked in London for much of his life.
Haydn, Joseph (1732–1809) Austrian composer. Kapellmeister at court of Prince Esterházy for nearly 25 years.
Holst, Gustav (1874–1934) English composer. An influential teacher, his large-scale works include *The Hymn of Jesus* and, most famously, *The Planets*.
Janáček, Leoš (1854–1928) Czech composer. Studied Czech folk music and wrote many operas including *Jenufa, Katya Kabanova,* and *The Cunning Little Vixen*.
Kodály, Zoltán (1882–1967) Hungarian composer who traveled around his country with Bartók, collecting and studying folk music.

Leoš Janáček

Liszt, Franz (1811–1886) Hungarian. Piano virtuoso, he rewrote many famous orchestral pieces for the piano.

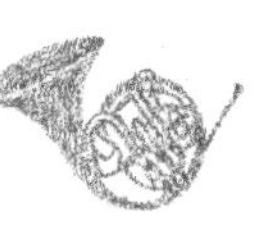

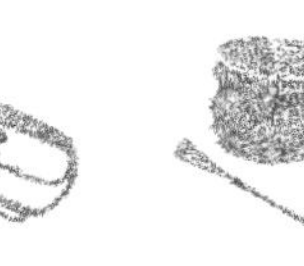

Lully, Jean-Baptiste (1632–1687) Born in Florence, Italy, Lully rose to become the foremost French composer of his day. Worked at the court of Louis XIV of France.
Mahler, Gustav (1860–1911) Austrian. Wrote ten symphonies and many songs.
Mendelssohn, Fanny (1805–1847) German. Overshadowed by her famous brother, she had a few pieces published in her own lifetime.
Mendelssohn, Felix (1809–1847) German. Composer and conductor, he revived many of Bach's works such as the *St. Matthew Passion*.
Messiaen, Olivier (1908–1992) French. Inspired by birdsongs, ancient Indian music, the Roman Catholic church. He wrote many large-scale orchestral works and much organ music.
Milhaud, Darius (1892–1974) French composer who was very much influenced by the rhythms and sounds of jazz music.
Monteverdi, Claudio (1567–1643) Italian. The first successful opera composer, his operas are still performed today.
Mozart, Wolfgang Amadeus (1756–1791) Austrian. Genius of the Classical period, he wrote many symphonies and operas including *The Marriage of Figaro* and *Cosi fan tutti*.
Musgrave, Thea (b. 1928) British. Studied with Nadia Boulanger. Has written several operas, including *Mary, Queen of Scots*.
Mussorgsky, Modest (1839–1881) Russian composer, friend of Rimsky-Korsakov. Most famous for his opera *Boris Godunov*.
Palestrina, Giovanni Pierluigi da (1525–1594) Took his name from his birthplace in Italy. Wrote over 100 settings of the Catholic Mass.
Poulenc, Francis (1899–1963) French composer and pianist. Wrote *Trois Mouvements perpétuels* for piano while he was serving in the army in World War I.
Prokofiev, Sergei (1891–1953) Russian. Pianist and composer. He wrote many symphonies, famous ballet music for *Romeo and Juliet*, and *Peter and the Wolf*.

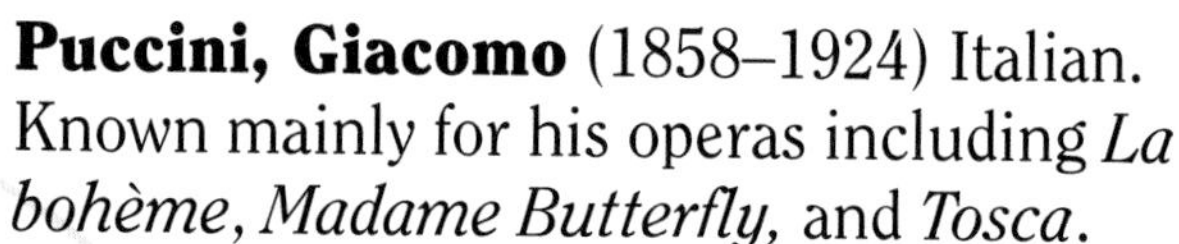

Puccini, Giacomo (1858–1924) Italian. Known mainly for his operas including *La bohème*, *Madame Butterfly*, and *Tosca*.
Purcell, Henry (1658–1695) English composer. Wrote church music, royal odes, and theater music including the opera *Dido and Aeneas*.
Rachmaninov, Sergei (1873–1943) Russian. Virtuoso pianist as well as conductor and composer. His most famous works include his piano concertos and symphonies.
Ravel, Maurice (1875–1937) French. Like Debussy, he was influenced by Indonesian gamelan music heard at the Paris exhibition. Wrote ballets, songs, and piano pieces.
Reich, Steve (b. 1936) American. Composer of minimalist music, he has worked with Berio and Milhaud and studied African drumming.
Rimsky-Korsakov, Nikolai (1844–1908) Nationalist Russian composer. Well-known for pieces such as the ballet *Scheherazade* and "The Flight of the Bumble Bee."
Rossini, Gioacchino (1792–1868) Italian. Opera composer, including *The Barber of Seville*.
Schubert, Franz (1797–1828) Austrian. Famous for his songs, often known by their German name "lieder," and chamber music.
Schumann, Clara (1819–1896) German virtuoso pianist, also a composer.
Schumann, Robert (1810–1856) German. Also famous for his songs, piano music, and symphonies.
Shostakovich, Dmitri (1906–1975) Russian. Wrote 15 symphonies as well as two operas and many film scores.
Sibelius, Jean (1865–1957) Finnish. Wrote music about the landscapes and myths of his country, Finland.
Smetana, Bedřich (1824–1884) Czech composer. Influenced by the nationalist movement and wrote pieces entitled *Má Vlast* (My Country) and *Vltava* describing the river that flows through Prague.

Sergei Prokofiev

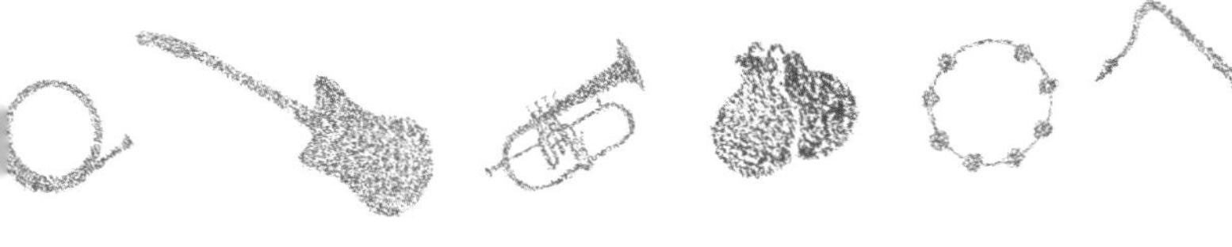

Smyth, Ethel (1858–1944) British. Famous for her opera *The Wreckers.*

Stockhausen, Karlheinz (1928–1994) German. Composer and performer of electronic music and works for orchestra, voice, and others.

Strauss, Johann, II (1825–1899) Austrian composer, known as the "Waltz King." One of a family of composers and conductors, he is remembered for his elegant waltzes such as "The Blue Danube."

Strauss, Richard (1864–1949) German. One of the most Romantic of the 20th-century composers and conductors, famous for operas such as *Der Rosenkavalier* and *Elektra*.

Igor Stravinsky

Stravinsky, Igor (1882–1971) Russian. Composer of *The Rite of Spring* as well as vocal pieces such as *Symphony of Psalms* and the ballet *Perséphone*.

Takemitsu, Toru (b. 1930) Japanese. Composes music with a mixture of Japanese and Western influences.

Tallis, Thomas (c. 1505–1585) English composer who was a member of the Chapel Royal with William Byrd. Wrote vocal music with both English and Latin words.

Tchaikovsky, Pyotr Ilyich (1840–1893) Russian. Romantic composer of many famous orchestral works including *Romeo and Juliet* and "1812" Overture.

Tippett, Michael (b. 1905) British. Composer of *A Child of Our Time,* which makes use of spirituals. Also wrote four operas including *The Midsummer Marriage*.

Vaughan Williams, Ralph (1872–1958) British. Made use of English folk songs in his music. Collected folk songs from 1903 onward.

Verdi, Giuseppe (1813–1901) Italian. Famous for his operas including *Aida* and *Rigoletto*. Also for his setting of the Requiem Mass.

Vivaldi, Antonio (1678–1741) Italian. Taught music at an orphanage in Venice and composed much music for his pupils including many concertos. Most famous today for his concerto *The Four Seasons*.

Wagner, Richard (1813–1883) German. Famous for his large-scale operas on mythological themes, especially the *Ring* cycle made up of the four operas *The Rhinegold, The Valkyrie, Siegfried,* and *The Twilight of the Gods*.

Walton, William (1902–1983) British. Wrote much orchestral and choral music including the oratorio *Belshazzar's Feast*.

Weill, Kurt (1900–1950) German composer who became an American citizen in 1943. Weill's operas combine cabaret-style songs with dialogue and orchestral music. They include *The Rise and Fall of the City of Mahagonny* and *Johnny Johnson*.

Weir, Judith (b. 1954) Scottish. Operas include *The Vanishing Bridegroom, A Night at the Chinese Opera,* and *Blond Eckbert*.

Franz Schubert (on the left) with musical friends.

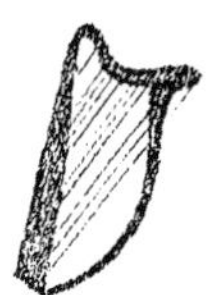

Index

    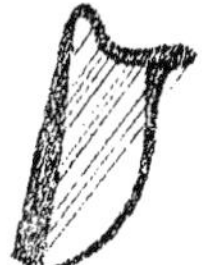